Allergy-Free Living

Asthma, hives, depression, headache, chronic fatigue, compulsive eating and drinking, insomnia, arthritis, hypertension, colic, retardation and epilepsy are just some of the physical and mental disorders that may be caused by allergic reactions to food.

Now, the allergy expert, Dr. Marshall Mandell, provides tested nutritional help for the treatment of food allergies, and vital health suggestions for allergy prevention. Emphatically, he states: "Being allergic does not mean you cannot eat delicious, satisfying meals."

And the wide variety of appetizing, wholesome dishes offered in this important cookbook proves it!

ABOUT THE AUTHOR

Fran Gare Mandell is best known as a coauthor of *Dr. Atkins' Diet Revolution*, *Dr. Atkins' Diet Cook Book*, and the *Super Energy Diet Cookbook*. She and her partner own Gare and Gadd, a Connecticut-based publishing company that researches and produces books about medicine and nutrition. Mrs. Mandell has a master's degree in biology and clinical nutrition. She is the wife of Dr. Marshall Mandell.

Dr. Mandell's
ALLERGY-FREE
COOKBOOK

Fran Gare Mandell, M.S.

Introduction by
Dr. Marshall Mandell

PUBLISHED BY POCKET BOOKS NEW YORK

The recipes in this book have been carefully researched
and tested. However, any persons considering a change
in diet should consult their doctor beforehand.

Another *Original* Publication of POCKET BOOKS

POCKET BOOKS, a Simon & Schuster division of
GULF & WESTERN CORPORATION
1230 Avenue of the Americas, New York, N.Y. 10020

Copyright © 1981 by Fran Gare

All rights reserved, including the right to reproduce
this book or portions thereof in any form whatsoever.
For information address Pocket Books, 1230 Avenue
of the Americas, New York, N.Y. 10020

ISBN: 0-671-83603-X

First Pocket Books printing November, 1981

10 9 8 7 6 5 4 3 2 1

POCKET and colophon are trademarks of Simon & Schuster.

Printed in the U.S.A.

*This book is dedicated
to Dr. Marshall Mandell
and the thousands of people
who are living a better life
as a result of his work*

We would like to thank the staff of Gare & Gadd, Inc.—Pat O'Malley, Francine Kydes, Barbara Bayuk, Janet Yellin, Sandra Richardson, Angela Michael and Kathy Bouton—for their valuable help in preparing this book. Thanks, too, for the assistance of Joan Jewell, Mary Francis Gullo and Angela Rinaldi.

CONTENTS

INTRODUCTION   *15*

1 QUESTIONS AND ANSWERS   *27*

2 WHAT TO DO IF YOU'RE
   SERIOUSLY ILL WITH
   ALLERGIES   *37*
   Fasting / *37*
      How to Prepare for Your Fast / *39*
      How to Fast / *40*
   The Rotary Diversified Diet / *43*

3 ABOUT THE RECIPES AND
   MENU PLANS   *50*
   5-Day Rotary Diversified Diet Menu Plans
      for Seriously Allergic People / *51*
      Samply 5-Day Rotary Diversified
      Diet / *52*
      Diet Chart Blank / *53*
   Menu Plans for Allergy-free Living / *55*
      6-Day Rotary Diversified Diet / *55*

Menu Plans for the Food-sensitive Person
    with Specific Food Allergies / 58
  6-Day Cane-, Soy-, and Egg-free Rotary
    Diversified Diet / 58
  6-Day Corn- and Wheat-free Rotary
    Diversified Diet / 61
  6-Day Yeast- and Milk-free Rotary
    Diversified Diet / 64

4 RECIPES   67
  Beverages / 67
  Dips, Dressings, Spreads, and Relishes / 70
  Soups and Stocks / 83
  Salads / 101
  Sauces / 107
  Meat / 116
  Fish and Seafood / 125
  Fowl / 132
  Vegetable Dishes / 136
  Eggs, Crepes, and Rice and Pasta
    Dishes / 147
  Pancakes, Muffins, and Biscuits / 159
  Breads / 170
  Cakes / 179
  Frostings / 185
  Pies / 191
  Cookies / 197
  Custard, Puddings, and Other
    Desserts / 203

5 USEFUL SUGGESTIONS   213
  Lunch-Box Suggestions / 213
  Allergic Tips / 215
    When Eating in Restaurants / 215
    When Going to Cocktail Parties / 217
    What to Eat on Holidays / 218
    College Tips / 219
  Nutritional Cooking Methods / 220
  A Glossary of Unusual Products Used in This Book / 221

APPENDIX 223

Hidden Food Allergens / *223*
Food Family Charts for Use in the Rotary
    Diversified Diet / *228*
  Plant Kingdom / *228*
  Animal Kingdom / *233*
Herb and Spice Charts / *237*

INDEX 245

Dr. Mandell's
ALLERGY-
FREE
COOKBOOK

Introduction

by
Marshall Mandell, M.D.
and
Fran Gare Mandell, M.S.

Food allergy is responsible for major medical and psychiatric problems. Eating foods that are not tolerated by different organs and systems of our bodies may result in the appearance of a broad range of physical and mental disorders. Hay fever, asthma, hives, eczema, depression, headache, chronic fatigue, compulsive eating, obesity, compulsive drinking, insomnia, hypertension, fluid retention, arthritis, duodenal ulcers, gallbladder colic, urinary tract symptoms imitating urinary infections, hyperactivity, learning disabilities, autism, retardation, multiple sclerosis, schizophrenia, and epilepsy only begin a list of disorders that may be caused by allergic reactions to foods.

Despite numerous well-documented case reports in medical journals and presentations given at scientific meetings around the world, food allergy is often ignored by the medical profession, nutritionists, and the general public as a major cause of disease. You may be surprised to know that illnesses resulting from even the most severe forms of food allergy may be unrecognized as disorders having their roots in people's diets.

Food allergies are often misdiagnosed because physicians, surgeons, psychiatrists, and pediatricians are not yet aware of the major role that food plays in the causation of these serious physical and mental problems. They believe many of these ailments are of unknown cause or are due to emotional stress. Even the most severe allergic brain dysfunctions are thought to be caused by some assumed but unproven form of "psychic trauma." Another frequent diagnosis for symptoms of food allergy is: "It's a virus infection." But probably the most common mistake physicians (including psychiatrists) make when diagnosing the symptoms of food allergy is to tell the patient he has a "psychosomatic illness."

When a patient is told he has symptoms for which there is no demonstrable physical cause, he often feels inadequate. He believes he has "imagined" the symptoms and begins to question his mental stability. Psychosomatic illness is a condition which is diagnosed too frequently on insufficient evidence. This situation must be rectified. Genuine illnesses related to food allergies are misdiagnosed. Treatments with drugs are not specifically directed to the underlying cause of the patient's illness—only to the symptoms.

The effects of food allergy do not fit a simple pattern. While certain foods will cause specific reactions in one person, these very same foods will cause completely different symptoms in others, or no apparent symptoms at all. Some people are much more sensitive than others; they react to foods that other people can tolerate in moderate portions.

That some people can tolerate what other people react to does not necessarily mean the food is harmless. People may not be allergic to foods, but their health may be affected by substances in them, such as artificial coloring and flavoring, preservatives, and insecticide residues. I believe that if a substance in a food is not good for some people, it is just not good for anyone.

In other words, if a person is not aware of any

food-related negative effects on his health, that does not mean the food is not harmful to his health. Most people recognize acute reactions to a food when a definite cause-and-effect relationship has been demonstrated a number of times. They are aware that each time they eat a certain food they get diarrhea or hives or a headache. After making this association repeatedly, they avoid these foods. But that is only the tip of the food-allergy iceberg. The most important type of food allergy is the form that causes a lot of trouble as it smolders along but remains undetected.

The daily exposure to a potential food allergen over an extended period can eventually lead to the development of an allergic state that causes a wide variety of mental and physical disorders. These disorders usually develop so slowly that the patient is not even aware that this subtle process is taking place. In time, the patient learns that something is wrong. The ingestion of food allergens over a long term has caused him to exceed his threshold of allergic tolerance. This allergic overloading causes symptoms to develop. Unfortunately, there is no suspicion, either by the patient or, in most situations, by his physician, that food played any role whatsoever in the development of the illness.

When a patient continues to eat a food that causes cumulative effects, the illness remains chronic and may become progressive. This chronic illness due to food allergy may be further complicated by food addiction, an extremely important and very common aspect of food allergy.

Like the alcoholic in his need for alcohol, a person who has a compulsive need to eat a particular food has become addicted to that food. Eating the food gives him relief from the symptoms caused by his last ingestion. It makes him feel better and may even impart a sense of well-being. It may also increase his energy level and make him more alert. But it is only a short time before withdrawal symptoms return again.

Unfortunately, again like the alcoholic, the "foodaholic" may not be able to get enough of his addictive food. The foods he is allergically addicted to tend to become his favorites. An inner need to relieve the symptoms that arise from ingesting those foods may precipitate eating binges. Many foodaholics wake up with monotonous regularity at 2:00 A.M. or 4:00 A.M. with a variety of symptoms like palpitations, itching, abdominal pain, diarrhea, joint pains, muscle cramps, headache, restlessness, or fear. What is happening at these early hours of the morning is that the food taken at suppertime is now causing a withdrawal effect on the body, including the nervous system. Food-addicted individuals have withdrawal symptoms similar to those experienced by alcoholics.

Many food-addicted patients have been misdiagnosed as suffering from a relatively infrequent disorder—hypoglycemia. These patients, in reality, are suffering from the delayed withdrawal effects of food allergy.

To complicate the serious problem of food allergy, modern technological advances in transportation, production, processing, and storage of food products (before their ultimate distribution to the consumer) play a very important role.

Today, most foods are something other than wholesome nutritional products of nature. They are "enriched," refined, processed, and preserved to increase their shelf life. They are artificially colored for eye appeal and artificially flavored for taste appeal. Advertising agencies have gone so far as to sell some nonnutritious beverages, such as diet soda, by capitalizing on sex appeal.

Foods are contaminated by residues of agricultural chemicals and by additives that enter the food during its processing. Some of the additives employed are unnecessary. Processing depletes the inherent value of food. Bran is removed from wheat flour and then sold back to us as fiber in order to repair some of the damage to our intestinal tracts caused by its absence. The germ is taken out of wheat and corn and fed to our livestock. We are deprived of this valuable substance, which is rich in vitamin E. It is ludicrous that the animals we eat are actually fed much better than we are.

When the processors "rape" our foods of vital nutrients we need for growth and repair of body cells, they go through the deceptive and criminal process of "enriching" foods. Though they return a small part of the nutritional values they remove, we never get the benefits present in the whole food. The food-processing industry is eliminating and changing inherent nutrients in our food supply. We are eating poorer materials because the essential materials we need from food are missing. As a result, we develop multiple vitamin and mineral deficiencies, predisposing us to the ravages of degenerative diseases. These diseases are responsible for 80 percent of our present mortality rate!

Before the food-processing industry plays its role in depleting and contaminating our food supply, the agricultural industry initiates the destructive domino effect. Chemicals (pesticides) are used to kill rodents; insecticides are used against insects; fungicides are used to control molds and parasites; and lethal herbicides are used to destroy weeds.

These residual chemicals are poisons. They permeate our foods. And we can't remove them by peeling or cooking. The livestock and poultry we eat are treated with such chemical agents as insecticides, antibiotics, hormones, tranquilizers, preservatives, and tenderizers. We continue to eat the foods anyway, despite laboratory studies that have demonstrated that these chemicals have produced cancer in animals.

Agricultural chemicals and additives become part of our food, and these substances build up in our bodies year after year. Man has survived the effects of these substances, but this does not mean they are harmless. Technological genius is outpacing the biologic capacity of the human body to cope with these dangerous materials.

Someday, people will look back on our days of "advanced" food technology with disbelief and say: "Those people must have been insane. They sprayed their food with poison, and then they ate it!"

The current state of our food supply represents a very serious problem for all of us. But for victims of poor health, or people who are overly sensitive to the effects of biologically active chemical agents present in food, the problem of contamination represents a serious threat to survival. People in poor health, in addition to being sensitive to those chemicals, become increasingly allergic and have less and less tolerance for them.

For some people, it is not always the food itself that causes illness. The food acts as a vehicle for the potentially harmful substances it contains. The food-related disorder is the susceptible person's reaction to various chemical agents that are incorporated in foods.

This is demonstrated by the patient who normally eats commercially grown fruits and vegetables and then switches to organically raised produce. The commercial produce causes symptoms that appear to be due to a food allergy. Actually, they are reactions to some of the chemical agents present in the food. We know this to be a fact because these people have no symptoms when they eat organically grown produce.

All of us learn from these sensitive people. As I said

20

earlier, if it is not good for some of us, it really cannot be good for anyone. We don't have to eat foods that are contaminated by chemicals. We don't have to eat foods grown in soil that has been depleted of some of its essential nutrients. Crops grown in soil subject to agricultural neglect are incomplete, mineral-deficient foods that are inadequate to sustain good nutrition. We must improve the nutritional value of these foods. We have no alternative.

Large yields of high-quality foods are being produced by organic farmers throughout the world. Like the Chinese, who have preserved soil fertility for countless generations, modern organic farmers are able to do the same.

Beyond food allergy, modern living imposes stresses that did not exist previously. Our bodies are assaulted and abused in many ways. Food allergy is only one of a continuum of closely related disorders that are due to the influence of countless environmental substances that people cannot tolerate.

There are harmful biologically active chemical substances in our water supply. As a result, it has become increasingly difficult to get a glass of pure water. Water from many of our streams, lakes, and even some wells cannot be trusted, due to increases in agricultural and industrial pollution. Fishing has been prohibited in many bodies of water because of serious degrees of pollution.

The air is unhealthy to breathe, outdoors and even in our homes. Modern chemical wizardry has produced innumerable products that contaminate our household air and make it unsafe for many of us.

The design and physical arrangement of our homes can cause health difficulties. The location and construction of the garage makes it possible for fumes emanating from an automobile or a lawn mower or from many stored substances to enter the kitchen or the playroom and even go through the walls or ceiling into the bedroom of a chronically ill person who reacts to these air pollutants. Many a physician is not aware that such petroleum fumes may be a major factor in the causation of an illness he has been treating for a long time with poor results.

I wrote about these environmental allergens and their detrimental effects on health in *Dr. Mandell's 5-Day Allergy Relief System*. If you have read that book, you are aware of how widespread the problem of allergy is and how many serious illnesses are caused by it. It is possible that you may have begun to help yourself by following the suggestions in the book for testing and treating yourself at home for allergies.

The *Allergy-Free Cookbook* is a natural sequel. The information in it can be of vital importance to you and the members of your family.

For everyone who is not seriously affected by food allergy—and wants to stay that way—the cookbook provides gourmet recipes and meal plans that go a long way in preventing the development of food allergies.

For the food-sensitive person with many known dietary allergies, I recommend the Rotary Diversified Diet, a technique developed by Dr. Herbert Rinkel, one of our greatest clinicians in the field of bioecologic illness and allergy. In many cases, food allergy is related to the amount of food consumed and the frequency with which it is eaten. It is possible to treat many cases of multiple-food allergy, and prevent the development of additional problems, by having the patient eat a wide variety of foods with each food eaten much less frequently.

The sample Rotary Diversified Diets (sometimes referred to as Rotary Diet or R.D.D.) in the *Allergy-Free Cookbook* consist of appetizing recipes and meal plans that can be applied to many individual problems because they allow you to make substitutions for the foods to which you are allergic. You are to eat each particular food only once every five to seven days. By rotating your exposure to each food in your diet, you allow the food to completely clear your body before you have a second exposure to it five to seven days later. This prevents a gradual buildup of the food which otherwise would have a cumulative effect in your body, a situation that can lead to many kinds of illness. Being allergic does not mean you cannot eat delicious, satisfying meals—especially if you do not have too many food allergies.

For the severely allergic person, first employ the original Rinkel Mono-Diet. This diet is a Rotary Diversified Diet, but you are to eat only *one* food at each meal. This diet has produced amazing results for many patients who have found it difficult or almost impossible to discover on their own (without testing in the office) the food (or foods) that causes them to feel poorly. By following the guidelines in this diet, many patients have been able to identify the culprits in their diets and begin to function more normally and lead healthier and happier "allergy-free" lives.

In addition to the recipes and meal plans in the *Allergy-Free Cookbook,* you will find other useful information to help you in preventing and treating food allergy through good nutrition. There are guidelines for fasting, and helpful charts that list hidden food allergens, and suggestions for the use of herbs and spices. Allergic tips, such as "Lunch-Box Suggestions," "When Eating in Restaurants," "When Going to Cocktail and Dinner Parties," "What to Eat on Holidays," and "College Tips," should make your journey to better health a lot simpler.

All of the foods in the meal plans and recipes should

be of high quality. Adding quality to the shopping list will require spending a little more money, but you will find it a wise investment. By buying high-quality foods, you will be giving your body, and the bodies of your loved ones, the best possible raw materials to sustain them. Good food is vital for the growth, repair, and production of new tissues and the manufacture of essential hormones and enzymes that are the very basis of life itself.

The *Allergy-Free Cookbook* is based on the use of whole, fresh foods—leaving out processed foods entirely. In many cases, you will start from scratch. You will find it easier (and a lot more fun) to prepare these fresh, natural foods. And as your taste buds awaken after years of lying dormant, you will discover that natural foods taste so much better!

Although our bodies are amazingly complex and miraculously resilient biochemical systems, we cannot violate the laws of nature indefinitely. We cannot afford to take a short-term view of the body abuse we are inflicting on ourselves when we continue to eat foods that are not good for us and foods to which we are allergic.

Fortunately, the results of many of our abuses are partially or completely reversible. We can quit smoking and our lungs may be able to repair themselves. But we can only salvage what has not been irreversibly damaged, and so the sooner we start, the better off we will be. There is a fine line between what the body may tolerate and recover from and the onset of permanent tissue damage.

The survival of man is a testimonial to his inherent resistance and vitality. We must stop sapping that vitality. Most of the population survive on diets of nutritionally incomplete and otherwise harmful foods.

They are alive but are not as vital, healthy, or happy as they could be because of allergy, poor environment and inadequate diets. As a result, they cannot reach their full potential—physically, intellectually, or emotionally.

The *Allergy-Free Cookbook* was written to help people become what they are truly capable of being by adopting an allergy-prevention or allergy-treatment approach. The proper selection and preparation of the nutrient materials in your environment, which eventually become incorporated into your body, is vital for good health. I am confident that for many of you this cookbook of nutritionally sound and appetizing meals will provide a new adventure in allergy-free living.

CHAPTER 1

Questions and Answers

by Marshall Mandell, M.D.

Question 1: What is a food allergy?

Answer: A food allergy is an illness resulting from eating foods your body cannot tolerate. Most people are not aware that food allergy is a major health problem that can lead to many types of physical and mental disorders. It affects about 75 percent of the population.

Question 2: What does the general public think food allergy is?

Answer: Most people associate food allergy with acute reactions to foods, such as itching, hives, headache, or intestinal upsets. Contrary to what the general public believes, these reactions, which occur shortly after eating a particular food, do not represent the majority of food allergies. They account for only 5 to 10 percent. The most common forms of food allergy are disorders due to the cumulative effects of frequently eaten foods, the withdrawal reactions of food addiction, and responses to various chemical agents that are used in food production and processing.

Question 3: Why is food allergy so common?

Answer: Food allergy is common because we eat every day. The effects of the foods in a single meal, and the chemicals associated with them, can last from three days to a month or longer. We eat two or three pounds of food in our three daily meals, and in a year we consume over 1,000 meals totaling from 700 to 1,100 pounds. This unending exposure is increased by snacks, after-school treats, coffee breaks, and midnight raids on the refrigerator.

Question 4: What physical disorders can be caused by food allergy?

Answer: Food allergy is often responsible for disturbances in the mouth, such as cold sores and inflamed gums, and stomach problems like ulcers and indigestion. It can cause gallbladder attacks and intestinal disorders such as ulcer, colitis, and gas.

Food allergy can affect the eyes, ears, nose, sinuses, throat, bronchial tubes, and lungs. It is a major factor in arthritis, causing pain in the joints, muscles, back, and neck. Food allergy causes headaches (including migraine), weakness, fatigue, palpitations, and severe itching with no visible skin problems. Headache, "growing pains," abdominal pain, bed-wetting, and hyperactivity occur in many allergic children.

All of these disorders can be caused by the foods we eat after they have been broken down in the digestive system and enter the bloodstream through the walls of the intestines. The circulatory system transports digested foods to all systems and organs of the body, including the brain (which has the richest blood supply of any organ). Allergic reactions to foods can affect the function of any organ or system and cause a wide variety of physical disorders.

Question 5: What mental disorders can be caused by food allergy?

Answer: An allergic reaction in the brain (cerebral allergy) may interfere with all of its functions, including intelligence, behavior, emotions, hearing, vision, and touch. Brain reactions may cause nervousness, restlessness, irritability, unprovoked anger, dizzy spells, lightheadedness, withdrawal, inability to concentrate, poor memory, learning disabilities, mood swings, psychotic behavior, and schizophrenia.

Question 6: If my doctor says my symptoms are psychosomatic, could they be caused by food allergy?

Answer: Yes. If you are ill and your doctor cannot detect any physical abnormalities and your laboratory tests are negative, there is a good chance that your puzzling symptoms may be caused by food allergy. If your doctor does not have a working knowledge of food allergy, he cannot possibly diagnose your illness correctly. He may tell you that you have a psychosomatic disorder—an "it's all in your head" condition—that is due to stress and you need a vacation. He may even prescribe a tranquilizer or antidepressant, or refer you to a psychiatrist.

Question 7: Are some foods more likely to cause allergic reactions than others?

Answer: Yes. The most frequently eaten foods in the diet are usually responsible for most of the symptoms due to food allergy. Recent surveys by allergists who specialize in food allergy identified milk as the leading allergic offender in children, and coffee as the major offender in adults. Wheat was the next most common offender in both adults and children.

Many physicians regard certain foods such as eggs, nuts, fish, spices, and chocolate as being highly allergenic. They advise patients to avoid them without evidence that any of these foods are actually responsible for a particular person's illness. Such advice may do considerable harm because many important food offenders may remain in the patient's diet. As a result, the patient may suffer because proper treatment is not received.

The following foods have been found to be the major allergic offenders. They are on this list because we eat them frequently and usually in large amounts: wheat, corn, oats, rice, rye, cane sugar, milk, beef, egg, chicken, pork, tuna, flounder, apple, banana, lettuce, tomato, potato, onion, string beans, soy, peanut, coffee, tea, chocolate, black pepper, paprika, and mustard.

Question 8: Can I become addicted to a food the way some people become addicted to drugs?

Answer: Yes. Addictive food allergy is in many ways similar to drug addiction. Just like the drug addict, the food addict will experience withdrawal symptoms—such as irritability, restlessness, headache, fatigue, or depression—a number of hours after the addictive food is ingested. In order to be comfortable, he must eat the foods to which he is addicted. On the other hand, he may actually crave certain foods and not realize he is a food addict. When an addictive food is eaten during a withdrawal reaction, withdrawal symptoms decrease in intensity or clear up entirely. This relief from eating is only temporary; reexposure to the food causing the original illness makes the withdrawal symptoms return.

As you can see, food addiction is characterized by repeated cycles of withdrawal symptoms and relief that are perpetuated by frequent ingestion of the addictive foods. Unfortunately, an overwhelming majority of practicing physicians see the effects of food withdrawal in countless thousands of cases of food addiction each day, but they do not even know that this serious condition exists. Most physicians whose patients suffer from food addiction do not realize that food is the cause of the illness.

Question 9: Could I have a serious illness due to food allergy and not know it?

Answer: Most definitely, yes. Cumulative allergic reactions to foods may develop slowly over a period of time. If you are allergic to a food and eat it two or three times a week, there is never a time when your body is free of that food, and it accumulates to a level that exceeds your tolerance. This results in a series of continuing allergic reactions in which one reaction begins before the previous reaction subsides. This often causes a serious chronic illness. Although you may be sick most of the time, you may never realize that your chronic illness is caused by cumulative food allergy.

Question 10: How can I test myself for food allergy?

Answer: The simplest method of testing yourself for food allergy is to avoid the most common offending foods in our Western diet and see how you feel. These foods are listed in the answer to Question 7. Make a list of the foods you eat infrequently (about once every five days). Try eating these foods in place of the offending foods on a daily basis.

If you follow this advice you will probably eliminate most allergic offenders and feel better. Under no circumstances should you eat any food that you love, crave, or have eaten on binges. Do not eat any food that makes you feel more alert or more energetic or gives you a sense of well-being. These responses to foods are all signs of food addiction, one of the most common factors in food allergy. (See Question 10 on food addiction.)

A more specific method of testing for food allergy is the Rotary Diet. Guidelines for designing and following a Rotary Diet can be found in Chapter 2 of this book.

Question 11: If I am allergic to a food, will I ever be able to eat it again?

Answer: Yes. In time you will probably be able to eat 50 to 70 percent of the foods you are unable to eat now. This reversible type of food allergy develops because we eat potential food offenders too often and become allergic to them. If we eliminate them from our diet for one to six months and give our bodies an "allergic rest period," there is an excellent chance that our tolerance to these foods will be regained. If it is regained, we must never forget that we became allergic to the offending foods because of exposure to them and that we will lose our regained tolerance for them if we again begin to eat them too often. In some patients, food tolerance is in a very delicate state of balance, and a brief period of "abuse" may cause a rapid return of allergic symptoms—sometimes in as little as one week.

Unfortunately, there are some food allergies that are "fixed," or permanent. In this type of allergy certain foods will cause symptoms even if they have been eliminated from the diet for several years.

Question 12: What can I do to control or prevent my allergic reactions to food?

Answer: There are several steps you can take to reduce your reactions to food. First, rest your body by avoiding major dietary offenders for one to six months, depending on the severity of your reactions to each food. Then, to see if they still cause symptoms, reintroduce these foods into your diet one at a time, eating the same food only once a week. For example, if you are moderately allergic to beef, do not eat it for two months and then test yourself by putting it back into your diet by eating it once a week.

Second, you can prevent the development of new

allergies by eating foods to which you are not allergic once every four to five days. By decreasing the number of times you eat a food, you will preserve your existing tolerance to it.

Third, minimize your biologic stress from environmental chemicals and fumes by avoiding them as much as possible at home and elsewhere. Eat natural foods that are free of agricultural chemicals and nonnutritive substances used during food processing. Drink pure spring water. It is not contaminated by chemical agents.

Fourth, build up your body's internal resistance with good nutrition. Eat whole grains and fresh fruits and vegetables. Prepare these foods properly, so the essential vitamins and minerals are not lost in the water during cooking. (See Chapter 5 for proper cooking suggestions.) Avoid refined foods, and get plenty of rest and exercise.

Question 13: Can vitamins and minerals decrease the severity of allergic reactions to foods?

Answer: Yes. The average diet does not provide adequate amounts of most essential nutrients because of food processing, cooking, and soil deficiencies associated with food production. For example, adequate amounts of vitamins C and B_6, and the mineral zinc, are not available in the modern diet. Some physicians employ nutritional therapy to build up their patients' health and make them less prone to allergies and other forms of illness. Many allergic patients have noted improvement in their condition as a result of better nutrition and vitamin/mineral supplementation.

Question 14: Can other allergies like hay fever and chemical sensitivities affect food allergy?

Answer: Yes. Allergic sensitivity to house dust,

molds, pollens, animal danders, environmental chemicals, and other allergens often make food allergy much worse.

During the hay-fever season, a latent allergy to any food may appear. The pollens that cause the hay fever combine with the effects of the foods, creating an allergic stress greater than our bodies can tolerate.

The combined effects of foods and chemical substances can cause similar problems. Symptoms from foods may appear upon, or be aggravated by, exposure to chemical stresses such as cigarette smoke, permanent magic markers, paint, insect sprays, hair sprays, furniture polish, and mothballs.

Question 15: Can alcoholic beverages aggravate food allergy?

Answer: Yes. Alcohol can aggravate food allergy because it hastens the rate of absorption of offending foods into the bloodstream and allergic reactions to the foods are more likely to occur. This effect is similar to the reactions caused by mixing alcohol with drugs. Everyone knows that if a person takes sleeping pills or tranquilizers and drinks alcoholic beverages at the same time, he will overreact to this dangerous combination. Similarly, when alcohol is mixed with an offending food, the alcohol will foster an allergic response. For example, when Mrs. Y. eats shrimp at home, it doesn't bother her. But when she eats it in a restaurant, she gets unexplained facial swelling, hives, and diarrhea. While Mrs. Y. never drinks alcoholic beverages with her meals at home, in restaurants she drinks a cocktail with her shrimp dinner.

Question 16: Is food allergy an important cause of illness in children?

Answer: Food allergy is a very important factor in many disorders of infants and children. In infancy it can be the cause of colds, restlessness, rashes, and intestinal disturbances. Older children may have allergic headaches, abdominal pains, and bladder problems (including bed-wetting), as well as joint and muscle pains, which are frequently misdiagnosed as growing pains. A major childhood problem caused by food allergy is hyperactivity, a disturbance often associated with learning disabilities and mood swings.

Question 17: Does heredity play a role in allergy?
Answer: Yes. The probability of having an allergic child is increased when one parent is allergic. It is even more likely that allergies will develop early in life if both parents are allergic.

A family history of allergy, however, should not be relied upon as a major factor in making a diagnosis of allergy. A child may be allergic even if neither parent has allergies. The same parents may have both allergic and nonallergic children. Each patient must be evaluated on an individual basis.

Question 18: What can happen if a food allergy is misdiagnosed?
Answer: When food allergy is misdiagnosed, the cause of the underlying illness is completely overlooked. This is a very serious matter affecting millions of people. Many unnecessary diagnostic procedures and treatments are implemented when food allergy is unrecognized. Unnecessary risks, discomfort, and expense are often incurred by the patient. It is unfortunate that so many cases of unrecognized food allergy are misdiagnosed as psychosomatic illness. These patients suffer needlessly because their condition is misinter-

preted as the result of emotional inadequacy or inability to cope with the normal stresses of daily living.

Patients with serious illnesses due to allergy remain unrecognized in most medical practices. Many of these patients could be helped a great deal by physicians who are aware of the bodywide effects of food allergy.

CHAPTER 2

What to Do If You're Seriously Ill with Allergies

FASTING

At first, you may be surprised to find a chapter on fasting in an allergy cookbook. After all, fasting and cookbooks don't seem to go together. There are, however, very good reasons for including this chapter. The most important one is that fasting, when followed by a series of food-ingestion tests, is the most accurate method of determining which foods you are allergic to. After that has been accomplished, you may be able to rid yourself of the distressing symptoms caused by your food allergy.

Fasting on spring water is the best way to cleanse your body of the food and chemical residues which have been building up over the years. When you fast, positive changes will begin to take place in your body. Your digestive tract will get a complete rest from its normal continuous activity. Fasting will also give your entire body, including your nervous system, a welcome respite from your present allergic reactions to food.

Fasting is an excellent way for you to prepare for the Rotary Diversified Diet. By eliminating all food for a period of five days—the usual time it takes for the body to free itself from effects of food allergens—you will be able to discover the symptoms that food allergies and chemical sensitivities have been causing. There may be problems if you do not fast and continue to eat foods to which you are allergic right up to Day 1 of the Rotary Diet. You probably will have such mild reactions to those foods when they are reintroduced into your diet that your symptoms may not be of sufficient intensity to convince you that any of the foods are causing reactions that affect your physical and mental health.

Fasting is an excellent way to test for the presence of food allergy because relief from symptoms demonstrates that food was responsible for your illness. If symptoms recur following the reintroduction of certain foods, you will have established a definite cause-and-effect relationship between those foods and your familiar symptoms.

Fasting is not as difficult as you may think. Many people who have never fasted imagine that they will experience a feeling of constant hunger. That is a common misconception. Initially, you will probably feel moderately hungry, but within a day or two your hunger will disappear. The reason for that is simple. Your body will quickly adjust to fasting and it will begin to utilize its own reserves to sustain you.

If your general state of health is reasonably good, you are probably a suitable candidate for fasting. But don't make this decision by yourself. **A fast should be undertaken only if your doctor feels it would be safe for you after a complete examination. If you have a serious illness like asthma, epilepsy, or diabetes, or a psychiatric problem that has caused you to harm yourself or others, you should fast only under a doctor's supervision in a hospital where there is constant medical care.** Thousands of people have fasted without any harmful effects, and the benefits of fasting have been reported extensively in the medical literature.

HOW TO PREPARE FOR YOUR FAST

The week before your fast, stock up on plenty of spring water from a reliable source. Spring water should be used because it is free of chlorine, flouride, industrial wastes, and agricultural chemicals that are often present in local water supplies. Don't buy spring water in plastic containers, because it may be contaminated by chemicals used in manufacturing the plastic.

After obtaining a supply of spring water, it is time to make your home environment as free as possible of allergens and chemical offenders. This is a very important step. Results from fasting will be greatly enhanced by controlling your environment. If you don't do this, the effectiveness of your fast may be greatly reduced or the results may be misinterpreted. Eliminating the burden of food allergy by fasting may alleviate your symptoms, but chemical factors in your environment, in addition to airborne allergens such as dust, mold, pollens, insects, or animal dander, can continue to make you ill during a fast. The following case report illustrates how this can happen.

One of Dr. Mandell's food-allergic patients, a young woman in her mid-twenties, fasted at home with no improvement. When she came to his office, her testing showed that many of her symptoms were caused by sensitivity to a number of reactive chemical agents as well as a number of foods. The chemicals had not been eliminated from her home prior to fasting, and they continued to cause reactions during her fast.

If you fast and feel a little better but still are not well, then food is only one of several factors causing your illness. Your exposure to environmental allergens and chemicals must also be controlled during fasting.

Here are some suggestions for preparing your home environment before your fast.

1. For bedding, use only pure, untreated cotton. Since most pillows are filled with synthetics or feathers, you should avoid them. Instead, stuff a cotton pillowcase with towels.

2. You must not smoke. Smoking is not allowed in your environment. Be sure your entire home is free of smoke before you fast.

3. Be certain that no chemical agents that produce odors or vapors—such as furniture polish, air fresheners, insect sprays, hair sprays, cosmetics, and disinfectants—are used in your home during your fast.

4. Avoid scented substances like soaps and shampoos.

5. Animals are not permitted in the house.

6. Have a collection of recreational materials on hand. But be sure they're old, aired-out books, magazines, games, and cards. Newer materials of this kind may contain active chemicals that are released into the surrounding air. For example, print in new books and on covers is made from petrochemicals, and so is the fixative for the print. New games often contain odorous, freshly manufactured plastics made from petrochemicals. Don't take any chances of contaminating your fasting environment. Remember, reactions to unsuspected allergens and chemicals in your home can greatly reduce the effectiveness of your fast.

Now you are ready to stop eating and start fasting!

HOW TO FAST

If you work from Monday to Friday, it is recommended that you start your fasting on a Thursday evening by skipping dinner and drinking spring water exclusively. If you begin your fast on Thursday evening, you should not have too much trouble getting through one day at work if you are not highly allergic to food. By starting on Thursday, you will be able to rest at home as you undergo the withdrawal symptoms that usually appear during the first few days of fasting.

During your fast, you will eliminate the food and chemical residues from your diet that are in your intestinal tract, and your kidneys will clear your blood of wastes. You can help your kidneys and intestines by drinking lots of spring water and taking laxatives and enemas when needed.

After your last meal, and every other day during your fast, take a mild laxative like unflavored milk of magnesia or magnesium citrate. Follow the directions on each bottle for laxative effect. In addition to the laxative, take a spring-water enema on the first day of fasting. Add one level teaspoon of baking soda or sea salt to one pint of spring water at room temperature. The enema can be repeated two or three times a day for the first few days of the fast if severe constipation is present. If during your fast you find you feel weak and listless or any of your symptoms reappear, a laxative and an enema may make you feel better.

Drink plenty of spring water. To wash out the food and chemical residues in your intestines and bloodstream, it is advisable that you drink a large volume of spring water, at least eight 8-ounce glasses per day. Be sure not to run out. Many fasters may be tempted to drink "just a little" tap water instead of going to the store for spring water. One glass of tap water containing chemical agents you are sensitive to can cause symptoms. This careless action can set you back several days because food testing must be postponed until the symptoms clear.

Do mild forms of exercise. Stretching, walking, and yoga are excellent ways to exercise when you are fasting. But don't overdo! Take it easy, and avoid all unnecessary stress to your body and mind. Meditation is often helpful during a fast.

Do not use toothpaste or mouthwash. Active chemical substances in toothpaste and mouthwash can be absorbed directly into your system from the mouth. Brush your teeth with baking soda or sea salt, and floss with unwaxed dental floss. If you get a film on your tongue, brush it with baking soda or sea salt. Bad breath can be a problem during a fast, but it will disappear once your system is cleaned out. Don't make the mistake of using tap water to rinse your mouth. Keep in mind that this is strictly a spring-water fast!

Avoid extreme changes in temperature like hot or cold baths and showers.

Keep in touch with your doctor. He will want to know how you are progressing. Weigh yourself each day, and record the results. You may lose three to five pounds during your fast. If you lose much more weight, that will be due to a loss of retained water; water retention is often caused by allergic reactions. In addition to wanting to know about your weight, your physician will be interested in your general condition and the symptoms you may experience. He can determine whether or not you should continue with your fast. Many people have received valuable moral support from their doctors during a fast.

Do not take vitamin or mineral supplements. Remember, you are fasting. Do not take anything other than spring water. It is possible for you to have allergic reactions to some components of multiple-vitamin/mineral products.

Stop taking all nonessential medications if your physician says it's O.K. If you can omit any medications during your fast, you will be a step ahead in working out your problem. Eliminating medications will create a more ideal internal environment for diagnostic purposes. Do not stop any essential medications. You must not discontinue prescribed treatments for diabetes, thyroid disorders, heart disease, epilepsy, or other serious conditions. Do only what is recommended by your physician.

Smoking is not permitted. A number of Dr. Mandell's patients have found fasting to be the perfect answer for finally quitting this unhealthy habit. Cigarette tobacco and the paper cigarettes are rolled in are loaded with all sorts of chemicals. If you are a habitual smoker, it is likely that you have an addictive allergy to either the tobacco or the chemicals. By eliminating most of the allergic and chemical factors contributing to your illness—the foods, beverages, chemicals, air pollutants, and airborne pollens, molds, danders, and dust—you may find that the improved and much healthier environment is the key to giving up smoking at last.

THE ROTARY DIVERSIFIED DIET

There is a simple and ingenious dietary method for diagnosing, treating, and preventing food allergy. Called the Rotary Diversified Diet, it was developed by one of the great clinical researchers in the field of allergy, the late Dr. Herbert J. Rinkel.

Hundreds of physicians have used this valuable method to help more than one million patients recover from physical and mental disorders caused by food allergy. Follow carefully the instructions in this chapter and you also will have an excellent chance to decrease, and perhaps eliminate, your own unnecessary suffering.

One of the great advantages of the Rotary Diet is that it eliminates the cumulative allergic effects of foods. As discussed in Chapter 1 of this book, if we eat a potential food offender two or three times a week, our bodies are never free of that food. Finally, it builds up to a level we cannot tolerate, and our reaction to the overload may cause and perpetuate a serious illness. The Rotary Diet eliminates the cumulative effects of allergic foods. It gives us a rest period from each food before we eat it again.

Another important benefit of the diet is that it enables us to find out which foods cause mild reactions or no reactions at all. That information is of vital importance to the person who has many food allergies, because he will learn which foods he can eat without worrying about becoming ill.

The Rotary Diet is also an excellent technique for preventing the development of new food allergies. You have already learned that people who suffer from allergies will develop new ones if they overload their systems by eating a food too often. The Rotary Diet helps prevent new allergies because it reduces the number of exposures to a food. You will see exactly how the principle of food rotation is applied very soon, but first I would like to point out one more very important benefit.

If you follow the diet, you may increase your tolerance of airborne allergens, such as pollens, molds, house dust, and animal danders, as well as environmental chemicals. That benefit occurs because the allergic stress caused by foods has been minimized, thereby allowing you to better cope with other factors. The reverse of this principle is also true. Better control of airborne allergens and environmental chemicals may make it possible to better handle some of your food allergies.

Now that you are aware of the benefits that can be gained from a Rotary Diet, you are probably eager to design one for yourself. Before we show you how to do this, it will be helpful if you prepare your body for the diet. Fasting while drinking spring water is the very best way you can do this. If you prefer not to fast for five days, there is another way you can clear your system of all the foods which may be making you sick. Limit yourself to three of the following foods for five days: lamb, rice, squash, pineapple, and sweet potato. These foods are usually tolerated by many allergic people. It is also possible for you to start your diet without any preparation at all.

At this point, you must become acquainted with the fundamental principles of the diet. In a five-day diet, you will eat three daily single-food test meals for five days and you will repeat the five-day diet several times.

During the first five-day period, you will observe your reactions to fifteen different foods, which will be tested one at a time. As you learn which foods are causing your problems, you will be able to introduce more foods into your diet. In most instances, you will be able to determine which of the fifteen foods are causing your illness by carefully observing your reactions for four hours after eating each food.

Now you are ready to select your test foods. The best way to do this is to make a list of foods that you eat daily and then add the foods that are hidden in various food products if they are not already on your list. Wheat, eggs, milk, soy, cane sugar, and yeast are the major hidden food offenders. Next, select foods that you usually eat two or more times a week; and, finally, add the foods you love or crave, foods that make you feel more alert, and those that give you a sense of well-being, the "good foods." As you have already learned, the "good foods" may be those you are addicted to.

If you still haven't come up with fifteen foods, select from the following list of major food offenders. The chances that these foods are major culprits in your illness are very high. They include corn, oats, rice, rye, milk, beef, chicken, pork, tuna, flounder, apples, bananas, lettuce, tomatoes, potatoes, onions, string beans, soy, peanuts, coffee, and tea.

Once you have selected all the foods you would like to test, make certain you learn the biologic families to which they belong. (This information can be obtained by referring to the chart in Chapter 6). This is very important because if you eat foods that belong to the same family during the same day or on successive days, you are subjecting yourself to the possible cumulative effects from a substance that may be common to all members of the same family.

In order to avoid this, record all your selected foods on paper under their appropriate family headings. Then be certain when you make up your diet that there is a space of at least one day between members of the same family. For example, if you have an orange for breakfast on Monday, grapefruit may not be eaten until Wednesday or Thursday. Both are members of the citrus family.

If you have any problem designing your Rotary Diet, refer to the sample diet on page 55. If you still have questions, you may write to me at 3 Brush Street, Norwalk, Connecticut 06850; enclose your diet and a stamped, self-addressed envelope. I will make any necessary corrections or suggestions.

After you design your Rotary Diet, you are ready to begin a new experience in eating. Some people feel so well when following this diet that they continue to follow and modify it for months or years. Of course, only you can make the choice after you have carefully tested your reactions to each food. In most cases, it is best to go through three complete rotations of your diet. By so doing, you will have absolute proof that some of the foods you have been eating are the real villains.

It is necessary to eat foods at least four hours apart to allow sufficient time in which to observe each reaction. If your last meal is at 6:00 P.M., and your bedtime is at 11:00 P.M., you will be awake and able to observe any reactions from the evening food.

Remember, you should record the details of all responses, whether negative, mild, or severe, so that you can evaluate the results of each exposure to food you have tested. It is a good idea to prepare a chart that summarizes the reactions that resulted from each food.

If a food causes a reaction, do not eat the next scheduled meal. Instead, wait until the food-induced reaction clears. Obviously, if you eat while you are reacting, you will be confused regarding the possible effects of the second food, and you may become even more uncomfortable if the second food should also cause a reaction.

Do not be discouraged if you have a reaction. That is priceless information. For the first time during the long course of your illness, you are finding out why you have been sick, and any reaction that makes you uncomfortable and persists a good part of the day should be regarded as a tool to help solve the riddle of your food allergy. The symptom may have puzzled your physician for a long time until you began to investigate the possibility that your condition was caused by a long-standing, unsuspected food allergy.

For relief of symptoms from a test meal, you may take two to four tablespoons of unflavored milk of magnesia or a level teaspoon of corn-free baking soda (sodium bicarbonate) in one pint (two glasses) of water. A good alternative for the milk of magnesia is citrate magnesia or unflavored phospho soda. Two tablets of

Alka-Seltzer Gold in one pint of water may be taken in place of the sodium bicarbonate. Do not take laxatives containing artificial coloring or flavoring. A low-pressure one-quart enema made with two teaspoons of baking soda or sea salt can also be helpful in relieving symptoms. Check with your doctor or pharmacist if you have any questions.

Here are some more guidelines you should follow to get the best results from your Rotary Diet.

1. In place of standard table salt, use sea salt, which is prepared from evaporated clean seawater. It is available in health-food stores.

2. Drink well or spring water bottled in glass. Dechlorinated tap water may be used occasionally, but it should be boiled for ten minutes or exposed to air in a widemouthed glass container for three days. It should not be stored in plastic bottles.

3. Use organic foods whenever possible. They are best because they do not have chemical contaminants, additives, or preservatives. Store foods in glass containers or foil. Avoid canned foods.

4. Juices from fresh fruits and vegetables are best, but if you buy juices in a store, choose unsweetened juices in glass containers.

5. Cold-pressed unprocessed oils that are free of preservatives are best for you. Many kinds are available in health-food stores. They include sunflower, safflower, peanut, almond, olive, rice, and avocado. If you react to a food with oil added, retest the food and oil separately. Oils must be rotated in your diet and used according to food families.

6. Under no circumstances should you use refined sugar. To sweeten foods, use honey, dates or date sugar, pure maple syrup, beet sugar, corn sugar, currants, Shiloh Farms pure cane syrup, raisins, or sliced banana. If you have a reaction from any of these

sweeteners, stop using them. Rotate sweeteners according to food families. Use no artificial sweeteners.

7. Do not use refined flour.

8. When you have established your Rotary Diet for several weeks, you may want to introduce single spices and herbs. Rotate them according to food families. Do not use mixtures like catsup, prepared mustard, mayonnaise, or sauces. Garlic, lemon, and lime may be used in rotation.

9. Refer to Chapter 5 for the best methods of cooking.

CHAPTER 3

About the Recipes and Menu Plans

After speaking to hundreds of allergy patients at my husband's clinic in Norwalk, Connecticut, and meeting hundreds more as we traveled the country talking to people about *Dr. Mandell's 5-Day Allergy Relief System*, it became clear to me that people thought being allergy-free also meant being deprived of exciting, delicious foods. A diet for allergy-free living seemed boring.

I know that is not true. Being allergy-free is not being gastronomically deprived. As documentation, Jill Bomser and I decided to write a book that would delight even the most finicky allergic gourmet.

The menu plans and recipes in this book are written with two specific groups of people in mind: those of you who are not seriously affected by food allergies and want to stay that way, and those of you who have specific foods which you know you are allergic to.

We have learned that food allergy is most likely to occur in people who eat the same foods all the time. The menu plans show you how to rotate a large variety of foods, foods prepared to please both the eye and the taste buds. You will find that you may eat many of your favorite recipes. The difference will be to learn to eat them once every six days instead of three times a week.

We realize that you are probably not going to prepare every recipe in our menu plans. Unless you are very ambitious, you will find the menu plans are more useful as a guide to planning your meals. They can be followed loosely and you will still get the same dietary results. For example, a meal plan may read:

Breakfast: Cantaloupe with fresh cherries

Lunch: Broiled or steamed oysters, lobster,
    or crab with tarragon
    Steamed artichoke or artichoke hearts
    Fresh strawberries

Dinner: Almond Chicken (duck, pheasant,
    or goose) with Lemon Butter
    (omit egg, use soy oil for butter)
    Steamed spinach
    Fresh plums and Brazil nuts

5-DAY ROTARY DIVERSIFIED DIET
MENU PLANS FOR
SERIOUSLY ALLERGIC PEOPLE

The following menu plans have been designed for the seriously ill allergic patient. They are best used after a fast to help you gain tolerance to foods you may have been sensitive to. They will also help you identify those foods which your body cannot tolerate.

Remember to eat pure foods—free of chemicals and additives.

SAMPLE 5-DAY ROTARY DIVERSIFIED DIET

DAY OF CYCLE	1	2	3	4	5
A.M. MEAL	Wheatena (grain) or brown rice (grain)	pineapple (pineapple) or grapefruit (citrus)	oatmeal (grain) or millet (grain)	melon (gourd) or bananas (banana)	oranges (citrus) or apples (apple)
NOON MEAL	broccoli (mustard) or squash (gourd)	string beans (legume) or sweet potatoes (morning glory)	potatoes (nightshade) or cauliflower (mustard)	carrots (parsley) or peas (legume)	tomatoes (nightshade) or beets (goosefoot)
P.M. MEAL	chicken (bird) or eggs (bird)	lamb (mammal) or beef (mammal)	sole (fish) or cod (fish)	turkey (bird) or duck (bird)	scallops (mollusk) or pork (mammal)

Note: *The food family is listed in parentheses under each food. After day 5, repeat cycle.*

This is a blank chart that you can photocopy and use to create your own Rotation diets.

5-DAY ROTARY DIVERSIFIED DIET CHART

DAY OF CYCLE	1	2	3	4	5
A.M. MEAL					
NOON MEAL					
P.M. MEAL					
FOODS AND BEVERAGES USED AT OTHER TIMES					

As you can see, you are offered many choices of foods. You may eat all of them or some of them, *but do not eat any food that is not listed for the day.*

If you like cantaloupe with strawberries for breakfast, then eat the strawberries and have the cherries as a dessert for lunch. If you want to make crab salad for lunch (with crab meat, soy oil, and tarragon), do that and have the broiled chicken flavored with lemon juice as a main course for dinner. In other words, you may change the order of the foods allowed that day, but you cannot make any substitutions of foods that are not allowed for the day.

We have tried to give you a delicious variety of tastes to choose from so that boredom will hardly be a problem. Take the time to try the recipes, even if you only make one complete recipe a day.

A unique aspect of this book is the listing of substitutions at the end of each recipe. The substitutions were designed to enable those of you who are allergic to a food, or who don't care for the taste of a food, or who need variety in your rotation diet, to prepare a recipe with a choice of ingredients. Simply follow the instructions for the substitution; for example, if the substitution reads, "Substitute eggplant for chickpeas," do just that. Everything else in the recipe remains the same.

Chapter 5, "Useful Suggestions," is designed to help you stay on your eating regime even when its versatility is challenged. It will tell you what to pack in your lunch box, how to eat at a restaurant, what to eat at a cocktail or dinner party or at a holiday meal. There are even useful eating suggestions for college students. We know that you will find these suggestions most helpful.

We advise you to look over the table of contents carefully before you begin to read the book. There are many helpful hints to assist you as you travel the road

back to maximum good health and allergy-free living.
I wish you a mouthwatering journey.

Fran Gare Mandell

MENU PLANS
FOR ALLERGY-FREE LIVING

These are menu plans for the healthy ones among us who want to stay that way. Actually, even though you are in good health and do not believe you are allergic to anything, using these menu plans may have surprising health benefits.

We all have small complaints: not enough energy, mild headaches, an ache or pain here or there. Following these menu plans may completely relieve such problems. You are sure to feel better and prevent many illnesses that might have otherwise affected you.

Recipes that can be found in this book have been marked with an asterisk *(*)*.

6-DAY ROTARY DIVERSIFIED DIET

DAY 1

Breakfast Buckwheat groats with fresh pineapple
Broiled flounder, sole, or halibut (with sunflower oil)

Lunch *Tabouleh Salad (use sunflower oil and wine vinegar)

Dinner Broiled lamb (venison, buffalo, rabbit) chops with rosemary
Steamed broccoli or cauliflower
Pears and filberts

DAY 2

Breakfast   Cantaloupe with fresh cherries

Lunch   Broiled or steamed oysters, lobster, or crab with tarragon
Steamed artichoke or artichoke hearts
Fresh strawberries

Dinner   *Almond Chicken (duck, pheasant, or goose) with Lemon Butter
(omit egg, use soy oil for butter)
Steamed spinach
Fresh plums and Brazil nuts

DAY 3

Breakfast   Oatmeal with maple syrup and cashews

Lunch   Broiled trout (shad or salmon) with safflower oil
Baked potato with chives and safflower oil
Fresh blueberries

Dinner   Broiled pork chops (ham or bacon) with mustard seed
*Baked Stuffed Apple (use chopped dates for raisins, use poppy seeds for sunflower, omit maple, omit cloves)
Mashed turnips

DAY 4

Breakfast   Fresh sliced peaches or nectarines with hazelnuts

Lunch   *Sweet Potato and Banana Soufflé (use water for milk, use allspice for cinnamon)

Dinner	*Borscht (use ½ teaspoon minced fresh or powdered ginger for scallions, omit sour cream) Scallops sautéed in olive oil with basil Fresh raspberries

DAY 5

Breakfast	*Spicy Millet Pudding (use honey for maple, use dried figs for raisins, omit cinnamon and clove)
Lunch	Avocado stuffed with tuna Pomegranate or papaya
Dinner	Broiled steak or hamburger or veal chops with horseradish (pure) Sautéed eggplant, string beans and leeks (use sesame oil) One of the fruits not eaten at lunch

DAY 6

Breakfast	Baked grapefruit with date sugar and/or chopped dates
Lunch	Raw (or steamed) mussels (clams, shrimp) with bay leaf if steamed Lettuce, celery, and *Jerusalem Artichoke Salad with lime Fresh apricots
Dinner	Roast turkey (or guinea hen or squab) with thyme or sage Steamed red or green cabbage with caraway seeds Baked acorn squash Persimmons

MENU PLANS FOR THE FOOD-SENSITIVE PERSON WITH SPECIFIC FOOD ALLERGIES

The following menu plans are designed for people who have one or more of the common food allergies. We have made use of the recipes in this book whenever possible.

Just because you have food allergy does not mean that you cannot enjoy delicious gourmet food every day of your life. You just must pick your foods more carefully than someone who is not food-sensitive.

These menu plans are an example of how you can eat! They use the two basic principles of rotating your foods and taking out of your diet foods to which you are sensitive. After you become familiar with our meal plans, we are sure that you can plan many delicious meals on your own using the recipes in this book.

For instant reference to all recipes created for your specific allergies, refer to the Index, where they will be listed under the headings of the specific foods (for example: Tomato, Rice, Corn, Eggs).

6-DAY CANE-, SOY- AND EGG-FREE ROTARY DIVERSIFIED DIET

DAY 1

Breakfast   Buckwheat groats with fresh pineapple

Lunch   Broiled flounder, sole, or halibut (with sunflower oil)

*Tabouleh Salad (use pearl barley for bulgur wheat, use sunflower oil and wine vinegar)

Pears and filberts

Dinner   Broiled lamb (venison, buffalo, rabbit)
            chops with rosemary
            Steamed broccoli or cauliflower
            Roasted chestnuts (whole or puréed)

DAY 2

Breakfast Cantaloupe with fresh chives

Lunch   Broiled or steamed shrimp or lobster
             with tarragon
             Steamed artichoke or artichoke hearts
             Fresh strawberries

Dinner   *Almond Chicken (duck) with Lemon
             Butter
             (omit egg and tamari, use peanut oil
             for butter)
             Steamed spinach
             Plums and Brazil nuts

DAY 3

Breakfast *Basic Wheat Bread with *Cashew
             Butter and maple syrup

Lunch   Broiled trout, shad, or salmon steak
             with safflower oil
             Baked potato with chives and safflower
             oil
             Fresh blueberries

Dinner   Broiled pork chops (ham steak or
             bacon) with mustard seed
             *Baked Stuffed Apple (use chopped dates
             for raisins, use poppy seeds for
             sunflower, omit maple and cloves)
             Mashed turnips

DAY 4

Breakfast   Sliced oranges with hazelnuts

Lunch   *Borscht (use ½ teaspoon minced fresh
              or powdered ginger for scallions, omit
              sour cream)
          Sautéed scallops (with olive oil and
              basil)
          Fresh peach or nectarine

Dinner   Roast goose (or pheasant) with sage
          Baked sliced sweet potato and banana
              with allspice
          Raw or steamed endive or escarole
          Fresh raspberries

DAY 5

Breakfast   *Spicy Millet Pudding (use honey for
              maple, use dried figs for raisins, omit
              cinnamon and clove)

Lunch   Avocado stuffed with tuna with
              horseradish (pure)
          Papaya, pomegranate

Dinner   Sliced, broiled eggplant with melted
              Parmesan or mozzarella cheese
          Steamed or sautéed string beans and
              leeks (with sesame oil)
          (one of the 2 fruit choices not eaten at
              lunch may be eaten for dessert)

DAY 6

Breakfast   Baked grapefruit with date sugar and/or
              chopped dates

Lunch	Raw (or steamed) mussels, clams, or shrimp (if steamed, use bay leaf)
	Lettuce, celery and *Jerusalem Artichoke Salad with lime juice
	Fresh apricots
Dinner	Roast turkey (or guinea hen or squab) with thyme
	Steamed cabbage with caraway seeds
	Baked acorn squash
	Persimmon

6-DAY CORN- AND WHEAT-FREE ROTARY DIVERSIFIED DIET

DAY 1

Breakfast	Buckwheat groats with fresh pineapple
Lunch	Broiled flounder, sole, or halibut (with sunflower oil)
	*Tabouleh Salad (use pearl barley for bulgur wheat, use sunflower oil and wine vinegar)
Dinner	Broiled lamb (venison, buffalo, or rabbit) chops with rosemary
	Steamed broccoli or cauliflower
	Pears and filberts

DAY 2

Breakfast	Cantaloupe with fresh cherries
Lunch	Broiled or steamed oysters, lobster, or crab with tarragon
	Steamed artichokes or artichoke hearts
	Fresh strawberries

Dinner	*Almond Chicken (duck, pheasant, or goose) with Lemon Butter (omit egg, use soy oil for butter) Steamed spinach Fresh plums and Brazil nuts

DAY 3

Breakfast	*Oatmeal with maple syrup and cashews
Lunch	Broiled trout, shad, or salmon steak with safflower oil Baked potato with chives and safflower oil Fresh blueberries
Dinner	Broiled pork (ham steak or bacon) chops with mustard seed Mashed turnips *Baked Stuffed Apples (use chopped dates for raisins, use poppy seeds for sunflower, omit maple and cloves)

DAY 4

Breakfast	Fresh sliced peaches or nectarines with hazelnuts
Lunch	*Sweet Potato and Banana Soufflé (use water for milk, use allspice for cinnamon)
Dinner	*Borscht (use ½ teaspoon minced fresh or powdered ginger for scallions, omit sour cream) Sautéed scallops (with olive oil and basil) Fresh raspberries

DAY 5

Breakfast *Spicy Millet Pudding (use honey for maple, use dried figs for raisins, omit cinnamon and clove)

Lunch Avocado stuffed with tuna
Papaya or pomegranate

Dinner Broiled steak, hamburger, or veal with horseradish (pure)
Sautéed, sliced eggplant, string beans and leeks (use sesame oil)
(One of the two fruit choices not eaten at lunch may be eaten here)

DAY 6

Breakfast Baked grapefruit with date sugar and/or chopped dates

Lunch Raw (or steamed) mussels, clams, or shrimp (if steamed, use bay leaf) and lime juice
Lettuce, celery, and *Jerusalem Artichoke Salad with lime juice
Fresh apricots

Dinner Roast turkey (or guinea hen or squab) with thyme
Steamed cabbage with caraway seeds
Baked acorn squash
Persimmon

6-DAY YEAST- AND MILK-FREE ROTARY
DIVERSIFIED DIET

DAY 1

Breakfast   Buckwheat groats with fresh pineapple

Lunch   Broiled flounder, sole, or halibut (with sunflower oil and rosemary)
*Tabouleh Salad (use sunflower oil and wine vinegar)

Dinner   Broiled lamb (venison, buffalo, rabbit) chops with rosemary
Steamed broccoli or cauliflower
Pear and filberts

DAY 2

Breakfast   Cantaloupe with fresh cherries

Lunch   Broiled or steamed oysters, lobster, or crab with tarragon
Steamed artichoke or artichoke hearts
Fresh strawberries

Dinner   *Almond Chicken (duck, pheasant, goose) with Lemon Butter
(omit egg, use soy oil for butter)
Steamed spinach
Fresh plums and Brazil nuts

DAY 3

Breakfast   *Oatmeal with maple syrup and cashews

Lunch   Broiled trout, shad, or salmon steak with safflower oil
Baked potato with chives and safflower oil
Fresh blueberries

Dinner	Broiled pork chops (ham steak or bacon) with mustard seed
	Mashed turnip
	*Baked Stuffed Apple (use chopped dates for raisins, use poppy seeds for sunflower, omit maple, omit cloves)

DAY 4

Breakfast	Fresh sliced peaches or nectarines with hazelnuts
Lunch	*Sweet Potato and Banana Soufflé (use water for milk, use allspice for cinnamon)
Dinner	*Borscht (use ½ teaspoon minced fresh or powdered ginger for scallions, omit sour cream)
	Scallops sautéed in olive oil with basil
	Fresh raspberries

DAY 5

Breakfast	*Spicy Millet Pudding (use honey for maple, used dried figs for raisins, omit cinnamon and clove)
Lunch	Avocado stuffed with tuna
	Pomegranate or papaya
Dinner	Broiled steak or hamburger or veal chops with horseradish (pure)
	Sautéed eggplant, string beans and leeks (use sesame oil)
	(One of the two fruit choices not eaten at lunch may be eaten here)

DAY 6

Breakfast   Baked grapefruit with date sugar and/or chopped dates

Lunch   Raw (or steamed) mussels, clams, or shrimp (if steamed, use bay leaf)
Lettuce, celery, and *Jerusalem Artichoke Salad with lemon juice
Fresh apricots

Dinner   Roast turkey (or guinea hen or squab) with thyme or sage
Steamed cabbage with caraway seeds
Baked acorn squash
Persimmon

CHAPTER 4

Recipes

BEVERAGES

Fresh Mint Cooler

   1 cup pineapple juice
   2 tablespoons cream
   1 tablespoon honey
   ½ cup orange sections
   3 fresh mint leaves

Place all ingredients in a blender and blend until smooth. Serve over ice.

- Substitute orange or grapefruit juice for pineapple.
- Substitute yogurt for cream.
- Substitute maple syrup or date sugar for honey.
- Substitute fresh pineapple or grapefruit for oranges.

SERVES 1

Yogurt Fruit Shake

 1 banana
 ¼ cup crushed pineapple
 1 cup yogurt
 1 tablespoon honey

Place all ingredients in a blender and blend. Serve over ice.

- Substitute peaches for pineapple.
- Substitute milk or ice cream for yogurt.

SERVES 1

Tropical Shake

 ½ cup fresh papaya
 1 small banana
 1 cup orange juice
 1 tablespoon honey
 Pinch of nutmeg

Place all ingredients in a blender and blend. Serve over ice.

- Substitute mango for papaya.
- Substitute pineapple juice for orange.
- Substitute allspice for nutmeg.

SERVES 1

Apricot Yogurt Shake

½ cup dried apricots, soaked
    overnight in ½ cup water
1 cup plain yogurt
2 tablespoons maple syrup
½ teaspoon almond extract

1   Drain apricots and reserve soaking liquid. Place apricots, yogurt, maple syrup, and almond extract in a blender and blend, adding reserved liquid to make desired thickness of shake.

- Substitute prunes for apricots.
- Substitute milk or juice for yogurt and leave out soaking liquid.
- Substitute vanilla for almond.

SERVES 2

DIPS, DRESSINGS, SPREADS, AND RELISHES

Cottage Cheese and Sour Cream Dip

1½ cups cottage cheese
½ cup sour cream
¼ cup scallions or chives, minced
sea salt and pepper to taste

Mix all ingredients together and serve chilled with raw vegetables, crackers, or bread.

- Substitute ricotta cheese for cottage cheese.
- Substitute yogurt for sour cream.
- Substitute red or green peppers for scallions.

SERVES 4–6

Guacamole

2 ripe avocados, mashed
juice of 1 lime
2 cloves garlic, minced
2 tomatoes, peeled, seeded, and
    chopped
chili powder to taste
sea salt and pepper to taste

Mix the mashed avocado with lime juice. Blend in garlic, tomatoes, and seasonings.

- Substitute lemon juice or 1 tablespoon vinegar for lime.
- Substitute minced scallions or ginger for garlic.
- Substitute 1 medium pepper, chopped, for tomato.
- Substitute curry powder or 1 tablespoon tamari (see Glossary) for chili powder.

SERVES 4–6

Hummus

1½ cups cooked chickpeas
2 cloves garlic, minced
3 tablespoons lemon juice
½ cup tahini (see Glossary)
2 tablespoons parsley, minced
sea salt and pepper to taste

1   Purée chickpeas in a food processor or with a food mill. Beat in other ingredients.

This is great as a sandwich spread or dip with raw vegetables or pita bread.

- Substitute cooked eggplant for chickpeas.
- Substitute scallions or onions for garlic.

MAKES ABOUT 2 CUPS

Tahini Sauce

½ cup tahini (see Glossary)
½ cup plain yogurt
1 small clove garlic, minced
1 tablespoon lemon juice
1 teaspoon tamari sauce (see Glossary)
¼ teaspoon cumin

Beat all ingredients together until smooth. Add a little water if a thinner consistency is desired.

This can be used as a sauce for steamed vegetables, pastas, rice, fish, or seafood. It is also good as a dip for raw vegetables or as a salad dressing.

- Substitute peanut butter or cashew butter for tahini.
- Substitute ¼–½ cup milk, buttermilk, or water for yogurt.
- Substitute chopped scallions, fresh ginger, or parsley for garlic.

MAKES ABOUT 1½ CUPS

Basic Vinaigrette Dressing

2 tablespoons vinegar
¼ teaspoon dry mustard (optional)
6 tablespoons oil
2 tablespoons minced parsley
sea salt and pepper to taste

Blend all ingredients together well.

- Use wine, cider, or rice vinegar, or substitute lemon or lime juice, or use half vinegar and half lemon or lime.
- Use olive, corn, sesame, sunflower, peanut, walnut, soy, or any other type of oil.
- Substitute chopped scallions, onions, garlic, chives, dill, or basil for parsley.

MAKES ½ CUP

Russian Dressing

1 recipe Basic Blender Mayonnaise
  (see p. 73)
½ cup Basic Tomato Catsup (see p.
  82)
¼ cup chopped pickles or relish

Blend mayonnaise and catsup. Stir in relish.

MAKES 2¼ CUPS

Basic Blender Mayonnaise

1 large egg
2 teaspoons vinegar
½ teaspoon sea salt
¼ teaspoon pepper
½ teaspoon dry mustard (or 1
  teaspoon prepared mustard)
1 cup oil
3 teaspoons lemon juice
½ teaspoon honey (optional)

Put egg, vinegar, salt, pepper, and mustard in blender container and blend at medium speed. With blender still at medium speed add oil very slowly until blended. Add lemon juice (and optional honey).

Refrigerate in a well-sealed container.

- Substitute ½ cup cubed tofu (see Glossary) for egg.
- Substitute lemon juice for vinegar.
- Substitute 1 teaspoon tamari (see Glossary) for mustard.

MAKES 1½ CUPS

Avocado Mayonnaise
(Dip, Spread, or Dressing)

1 recipe Basic Blender Mayonnaise
  (see p. 73)
1 small ripe avocado

Mash avocado and place in blender container. Add mayonnaise and blend.

MAKES ABOUT 2 CUPS

Cashew Butter Mayonnaise

½ cup cashews
1 teaspoon mustard or ¼ teaspoon
  mustard seed
½ cup oil
2 tablespoons lemon juice
1 clove minced garlic (optional)
½ teaspoon celery salt

Place cashews and mustard in a food processor or blender and purée until smooth. Slowly add oil, continuing to blend. Blend in lemon juice, garlic, and celery salt.

- Substitute peanuts (or peanut butter) or tahini (see Glossary) for cashews.
- Substitute ½ teaspoon minced fresh (or powdered) ginger for mustard.
- Substitute cider or rice vinegar for lemon.
- Substitute sea salt for celery salt.

MAKES ABOUT 1 CUP

Curried Mayonnaise (Dip, Spread, or Dressing)

1 recipe Basic Blender Mayonnaise
  (see p. 73)
1 tablespoon curry powder (more or
  less to taste)

1 Beat curry powder into mayonnaise until well blended.

MAKES 1½ CUPS

Mustard Mayonnaise
(Dip, Spread, or Dressing)

1 recipe Basic Blender Mayonnaise
(see p. 73)
1 tablespoon prepared mustard (more
or less to taste)

Beat mustard into mayonnaise until well blended.

MAKES 1½ CUPS

Tofu Cream Cheese

6 ounces tofu, drained (see Glossary)
1 tablespoon safflower oil
½ teaspoon sea salt *Braggs salt*
dash of pepper
½ teaspoon lemon juice *or vinegar +*

Place all ingredients in a blender or food processor
and purée.

• This is a dairy-free substitute for cream cheese.

MAKES ABOUT 1 CUP

Tofu Sour Cream

    2 cups water
    ½ teaspoon sea salt
    8 ounces tofu (see Glossary)
    2 layers of 12″ by 12″ cheesecloth
    1 tablespoon lemon juice
    ¼ teaspoon sea salt

Bring water to a boil. Add salt. Drop tofu in and return to a boil. Remove pan from heat and allow to sit for 3 minutes. Remove tofu with a slotted spoon and place in center of cheesecloth. Pull four corners of cheesecloth up, twist them tight, and squeeze all excess moisture from tofu.

Place tofu, lemon juice, and salt in a blender container or food processor and purée until smooth.

This is a dairy-free substitute for sour cream.

MAKES ABOUT 1 CUP

Tofu Yogurt

    12 ounces tofu (see Glossary)
    2 tablespoons honey
    ¼ teaspoon sea salt
    ½ teaspoon vanilla extract

Place all ingredients in a blender or food processor. Serve with fresh or dried fruit, or jam.

This is a dairy-free substitute for yogurt.

• Substitute maple syrup for honey.
• Substitute frozen orange juice concentrate for vanilla.

MAKES 1½ CUPS

Apple Butter

2 pounds crisp, tart apples (such as
  Granny Smith)
2 cups apple cider
¼ cup maple syrup
2 tablespoons lemon juice
1 tablespoon lemon rind, grated
2 teaspoons cinnamon
1 teaspoon cloves
1 teaspoon allspice

Wash and quarter apples. Place in a heavy-bottomed
pot with cider and cook slowly until soft, adding more
cider if necessary. Put through a strainer or food mill.

Return to pot and add syrup, lemon juice and rind,
and spices. Continue to cook slowly, stirring often,
until mixture is a thick, spreadable consistency.

- Substitute peaches or apricots for apples.
- Substitute any juice for cider.
- Substitute orange or lime for lemon.

MAKES 3 CUPS

Peanut Butter, Banana, and Tofu Spread

¼ cup peanut butter
1 medium banana
6 ounces tofu (see Glossary)
1 tablespoon lemon juice
1 tablespoon honey

Place all ingredients in a blender or food processor and purée.

Use as a sandwich spread, a dip for fresh fruit, or a topping for ice cream.

- Substitute cashew butter or tahini (see Glossary) for peanut butter.
- Substitute 3 tablespoons of any fruit jam for banana and eliminate honey.
- Substitute maple syrup for honey.

MAKES ABOUT 1 CUP

Tamari Almonds

1 pound raw, unsalted almonds
(available at health-food stores)
¼ cup tamari (see Glossary)

Sauté almonds in tamari in a large skillet over medium heat until all liquid is absorbed and almonds are evenly coated.

- Substitute raw peanuts, cashews, or any other nuts for almonds.

MAKES 8 2-OUNCE SERVINGS

Apple Chutney

5 cups crisp, tart apples, peeled and
   chopped
2 cups apple cider
1 large onion, chopped
1 cup raisins
¼ cup lemon juice
2 tablespoons lemon rind
1 cup maple syrup
2 teaspoons ginger
2 teaspoons cinnamon
1 teaspoon clove

Place all ingredients in a heavy-bottomed pot and simmer just until apples and onions are tender.

This chutney goes well with pork, lamb, beef, cold meats, and cheeses. It is also great with cream cheese in an omelet or on a sandwich.

- Substitute pears or green tomatoes for apples.
- Substitute orange juice for apple cider.
- Substitute honey for maple syrup.

MAKES 1 QUART

Corn Chutney

2 cups corn
1 green pepper, chopped
1 red pepper, chopped
1 medium onion, chopped
1 cup apple cider
2 tablespoons vinegar

½ cup honey
1 tablespoon mustard
1 teaspoon cumin

Place all ingredients in a heavy-bottomed pot and simmer for 1 hour.

This chutney goes well with cold meats and cheeses, hamburgers, and meat loaf. Also try it on a grilled cheese sandwich.

- Substitute more peppers and onions for corn.
- Substitute lemon juice for vinegar.
- Substitute allspice for cumin.

MAKES ABOUT 3 CUPS

Raw Cranberry-Orange Relish

2 cups raw cranberries
2 tablespoons orange rind
1 cup orange sections
1 cup maple sugar or syrup

Grind cranberries in a food processor until finely minced. Add orange rind and sections and maple sugar or syrup and combine with cranberries. Refrigerate, covered, for 2 days before using.

- Substitute blueberries for cranberries (can be served immediately).
- Substitute lemon or lime rind for orange.
- Substitute apples for oranges.
- Substitute turbinado sugar or ½ cup honey for maple sugar or syrup.

MAKES ABOUT 4 CUPS

Basic Tomato Catsup

2 pounds tomatoes, quartered
1 medium onion, minced
4 tablespoons honey
½ cup cider vinegar
½ teaspoon celery salt
1 teaspoon sea salt
½ teaspoon pepper

Place all ingredients in a heavy-bottomed pot and simmer until tomatoes are very soft. Put through a strainer or food mill and return liquid to pot. Continue to simmer, stirring often, until catsup reaches desired thickness.

- Substitute 4 cups rhubarb for tomatoes (use more honey if needed).
- Substitute chopped green pepper for onion.
- Substitute lemon juice for vinegar.

MAKES ABOUT 1 CUP

SOUPS AND STOCKS

Basic Beef Stock

    3 quarts beef and bones, chopped into
       3-inch pieces (meat can be raw or
       cooked)
    cold water
    1 cup onions, sliced
    2 medium carrots, scraped
    ½ cup celery and celery leaves,
       chopped
    1 bay leaf
    3 sprigs parsley or 1 tablespoon dried
       parsley flakes
    6 whole peppercorns
    sea salt to taste

   Place beef and bones in a large stockpot and cover
with cold water by 2 inches. Add onions, carrots,
celery, bay leaf, parsley, peppercorns, and salt. Bring
slowly to a simmer and simmer gently, partially covered, for at least 5 hours, occasionally skimming off the
scum that accumulates on the surface.

- Substitute lamb, venison, beef buffalo, or any
  meat.
- Substitute sliced zucchini for carrots.
- Substitute thyme, rosemary, or marjoram for
  parsley.

MAKES 2 QUARTS

Borscht

1 pound cooked beets
2 cups beet juice
½ cup orange juice
½ cucumber, chopped
3 scallions, chopped
2 tablespoons fresh chopped dill
sea salt and pepper to taste
sour cream for garnish

Purée beets in a food processor or by pushing them through a sieve. Blend in juices. Add other ingredients. Serve cold, garnished with sour cream.

- Substitute carrots for beets.
- Substitute carrot juice or any type of stock for beet juice.
- Substitute zucchini for cucumber.
- Substitute juice of ½ lemon or 2 tablespoons cider vinegar for orange juice.
- Substitute chives, parsley, or basil for dill.
- Substitute yogurt or Tofu Sour Cream (see p. 77) for sour cream.

SERVES 4

Hearty Cabbage Soup

2–4 tablespoons butter or oil
2 medium onions, chopped
2 carrots, sliced
2 pounds cabbage, sliced

3 cups diced potatoes
2 quarts Basic Beef Stock (see p. 83)
½ teaspoon thyme
1 tablespoon parsley
sea salt and pepper to taste

Heat butter or oil in a stockpot. Sauté onions until tender. Add carrots, cabbage, and potatoes and cook until golden brown. Add stock and bring to a simmer. Add herbs and simmer for 1 hour. Season to taste.
This soup can be frozen.

- Substitute chicken, vegetable, or garlic stock for beef stock.
- Substitute brown rice, barley, or millet for potatoes.
- Substitute celery for carrots
- For a meal-in-itself soup, add leftover meat or fowl.

SERVES 6–8

Carrot Soup

3 cups carrots, sliced and steamed
   until tender
1 recipe Basic Potato Soup (see p. 96)
1 teaspoon cumin
sea salt to taste
chopped fresh parsley for garnish

Purée steamed carrots and blend with potato soup. Add seasonings. Garnish with parsley.
This can be served either hot or cold.

- Substitute 3 cups cooked turnips, pumpkin, or sweet potato for carrots.
- Substitute curry powder, dill, or anise for cumin.

SERVES 6

Chestnut Soup

1 pound raw chestnuts
cold water
1 medium onion, quartered
3 sprigs parsley
1 teaspoon thyme
cold water
2 cups chicken broth
½ cup heavy cream
1 teaspoon celery salt
sea salt and pepper to taste

Cut a cross on flat side of each chestnut with a sharp knife. Place chestnuts in a pot and cover with water. Bring to a boil; lower heat and simmer for 15 minutes until shells and skins can be removed easily.

Put peeled chestnuts, onion, and herbs in a pot. Cover with cold water and bring to a boil. Lower heat and simmer for about a half hour until chestnuts are soft and crumbly. Drain chestnuts and put them through a sieve, or place a few at a time in a blender or food processor. Slowly blend in chicken broth and cream until soup is a smooth, creamy consistency. Season with celery salt, sea salt, and pepper.

- Substitute almonds for chestnuts.
- Substitute 3 stalks celery, with tops, for onion.
- Substitute yogurt for cream.

SERVES 4–6

Basic Chicken Stock

2–4 tablespoons butter or oil
1 large onion, chopped
1 carrot, sliced
2 stalks celery with leaves, chopped
chicken neck, gizzard, heart, and/or
   chicken carcass and scraps
cold water
1 teaspoon parsley
1 teaspoon basil
2 teaspoons celery salt
sea salt and pepper to taste

Heat butter or oil in a heavy-bottomed 2-quart saucepan. Sauté onion until tender. Add carrot, celery, and chicken parts and sauté until golden brown. Cover these ingredients by 2 inches with cold water. Add herbs and simmer, partially covered, for 1½ hours or more, skimming when necessary. Add salt and pepper to taste. Strain broth and refrigerate. When broth is cold, fat will rise to surface and may then be skimmed off.

This stock may be frozen.

- Substitute any fowl, such as duck, goose, pheasant, or quail, for chicken.
- Substitute sliced zucchini for carrots or celery.
- Substitute marjarom or thyme for parsley or basil.

MAKES 2 QUARTS

Chicken Noodle Soup

2–4 tablespoons butter or oil
1 large onion, chopped
2 stalks celery, chopped
2 carrots, sliced
1 pound boned chicken
1 recipe Basic Chicken Stock (see p. 87)
1 tablespoon parsley
1 teaspoon basil
1 teaspoon celery salt
sea salt and pepper to taste
1 cup uncooked noodles

Heat butter or oil in a heavy-bottomed 2-quart sauce-pan. Sauté onion until tender. Add celery, carrots, and boned chicken pieces. Sauté until golden brown. Add chicken stock, herbs, and celery salt and bring to a gentle simmer. Simmer for 1 hour. Remove chicken; cut into small pieces. Add noodles and cook 10–12 minutes. Return chicken to soup. Add salt and pepper to taste.

- Substitute turkey broth and turkey meat or any other fowl, such as pheasant, goose, duck, or quail, for chicken.
- Substitute sliced zucchini for carrots.
- Substitute brown rice, millet, or barley for noodles.
- Substitute any meat or fish stock for chicken stock.

SERVES 6–8

Chili Bean Soup

3 cups cooked lentils or kidney beans
1 recipe Basic Potato Soup (see p. 96)
chili powder to taste
sea salt and pepper to taste

Add cooked beans to potato soup. Season and cook for 10 minutes.
This soup can be frozen.

- Substitute navy beans or pinto beans for lentils or kidney beans.
- Substitute curry powder for chili powder.

SERVES 6

Corn Cheddar Chowder

3 or 4 ears fresh corn, steamed
    (remove kernels), or 1 package
    frozen corn, steamed
1 cup grated cheddar cheese
1 recipe Basic Potato Soup (see p. 96)
1 red pepper, chopped
1 green pepper, chopped
1 teaspoon celery salt
chopped fresh parsley for garnish

Add corn and cheese to potato soup. Stir in peppers and celery salt. Cook for 10 minutes. Garnish with parsley.

- Substitute celery for corn.
- Substitute any cheese, or yogurt, for cheddar cheese.
- Substitute onion for peppers.

SERVES 6

Cold Cucumber Tapioca Soup

2 medium cucumbers, peeled, seeded,
  and chopped
1 medium red onion, chopped fine
4 cups Basic Chicken Stock (see p. 87)
2 tablespoons tapioca
2 tablespoons fresh chopped dill
1 teaspoon celery salt
yogurt for garnish

Place cucumber, onion, and stock in a saucepan. Add tapioca and bring to a boil, stirring constantly. Remove from heat. Add dill and celery salt. Chill and garnish with yogurt.

- Substitute 4 tomatoes for cucumbers.
- Substitute green pepper for onion.
- Substitute any type of stock for chicken.
- Substitute parsley, basil, or scallions for dill.
- Substitute sour cream of Tofu Sour Cream (see p. 77) for yogurt.

SERVES 4

Basic Fish Stock

2–4 tablespoons butter or oil
1 large onion, sliced
1 large carrot, sliced
2 stalks celery, chopped
3 pounds fresh fish, fish bones, or fish
    heads (flounder or halibut is
    recommended)
1 teaspoon lemon juice
1 bay leaf
4 sprigs fresh parsley or 1 tablespoon
    dried parsley flakes
4 whole peppercorns
cold water
sea salt and pepper to taste

Heat butter or oil in a heavy-bottomed 2-quart sauce-pan. Sauté onion until tender. Add carrot and celery and sauté until golden brown. Add fish, lemon juice, herbs, and peppercorns and cover with cold water by 2 inches.

Bring slowly to a simmer over moderate heat, skimming when necessary. Simmer gently for 30 minutes. Remove from heat. Add salt and pepper to taste. Strain and refrigerate.

This stock may be frozen.

- Substitute any seafood such as shrimp, clams, lobster, or mussels for fish.
- Substitute basil for parsley.

MAKES ABOUT 1 QUART

Garbanzo Bean Soup

½ pound dried garbanzo beans
   (chickpeas)
cold water
¼ teaspoon rosemary
2 tablespoons butter or oil
1 medium onion, chopped
2 cloves garlic, minced
2 tablespoons tamari (see Glossary)
2 tablespoons lemon juice

Cover beans with water and soak overnight. Add more water to cover, if necessary. Add rosemary and bring to a boil. Lower heat and simmer for about 2 hours until beans are tender.

Heat butter or oil in a skillet and sauté onion until tender. Add garlic and sauté for 2 minutes. Set aside.

Strain beans and reserve cooking liquid. Place beans (or half the beans, if you want a chunkier soup), onion, garlic, tamari, and lemon juice in a food processor and purée, using any cooking liquid to thin the soup to the desired consistency. (Stir in any reserved whole beans.)

- Substitute dried split peas or black beans for garbanzos.
- Substitute marjoram or basil for rosemary.
- Substitute green pepper for garlic and/or onion.
- Substitute sea salt for tamari.
- Substitute cider vinegar for lemon juice.

SERVES 2–4

Basic Garlic Stock

1 cup water
1 head garlic, separated (about 15
    cloves), unpeeled
1 quart water
6 peppercorns
1 bay leaf
1 tablespoon parsley
2 tablespoons olive oil
sea salt to taste

Bring 1 cup water to a boil in a small saucepan. Drop unpeeled garlic cloves in and boil for 1 minute. Drain. Run cold water over them and peel.

Bring 1 quart water to a simmer in a large saucepan. Drop in peeled garlic cloves, peppercorns, bay leaf, parsley, and olive oil. Simmer slowly for 30 minutes. Strain broth, pressing all liquid out of the garlic cloves. Add sea salt to taste.

This stock can be frozen.

MAKES 1 QUART

French Garlic Soup

3 egg yolks
4 tablespoons olive oil
1 recipe Basic Garlic Stock (see p. 93)

Place egg yolks in a soup tureen. Beat yolks with a wire whisk until thick. Beat in olive oil drop by drop as you would for making mayonnaise. Beat 1 cupful hot garlic stock into yolks. Then beat in rest of stock and serve immediately.

This soup cannot be reheated.

MAKES 1 QUART

Minestrone

2 tablespoons butter or oil
1 large onion, chopped
3 large carrots, sliced
2 stalks celery, chopped
3 fresh tomatoes, chopped
3 tablespoons Basic Tomato Paste (see p. 108)
1 cup cooked navy beans
6 cups Basic Chicken Stock (see p. 87)
1 teaspoon celery seed
1 teaspoon oregano
1 teaspoon fresh or dried basil
1 tablespoon parsley
sea salt and pepper to taste
2 cups cooked macaroni or noodles
½ cup grated Parmesan or Romano cheese for garnish

Heat butter or oil in a large stockpot. Sauté onion slowly until tender. Add carrots and celery and cook until golden brown. Add tomatoes and tomato paste and stir to blend with other ingredients. Add beans and stir. Slowly add stock while stirring. Add herbs and seasonings. Cook for about 20 minutes until vegetables are tender but not mushy. Add cooked macaroni. Garnish with cheese.

- Substitute 1 tablespoon cider vinegar for onion.
- Substitute parsnips or turnips for carrots.
- Substitute any type of beans for navy.
- Substitute any type of broth or tomato juice for chicken stock.
- Substitute brown rice, barley, or millet for macaroni or noodles.

SERVES 6-8

Onion Soup

3-4 tablespoons oil and/or butter
4 cups onions, thinly sliced
1 teaspoon honey (optional)
3 tablespoons unbleached or whole wheat flour
6 cups Basic Beef Stock, boiling (see p. 83)
sea salt and pepper to taste
4 buttered toast rounds
4 tablespoons grated Swiss cheese

Heat butter and/or oil in a heavy-bottomed 3-quart saucepan and sauté onions slowly for 15 minutes. Stir in optional honey and cook for 20 to 30 minutes, stirring often, until onions are a deep golden brown. Add flour and stir for 3 minutes. Remove from heat and add boiling beef stock, stirring constantly until thickened and smooth. Simmer, partially covered, for a half hour.

Season to taste. Ladle soup into ovenproof bowls. Place buttered toast rounds or crackers on top. Sprinkle with grated cheese. Place under broiler until bubbly.

- Substitute potato starch for whole wheat flour.
- Substitute chicken or vegetable stock or, for a richer, creamy textured onion soup, Basic Potato Soup (see p. 96) for stock.

SERVES 4–6

Basic Potato Soup

2–4 tablespoons butter or oil
3 cups sliced leeks or onions
3 cups diced potatoes
2 quarts water, Basic Beef Stock,
   Basic Chicken Stock, or Basic
   Vegetable Stock (see p. 99)
sea salt and pepper to taste

Heat butter or oil in a large skillet and sauté leeks or onions and potatoes until golden brown. Bring water or stock to a boil in a stockpot and add sautéed vegetables. Simmer for a half hour. Remove vegetables from broth and purée in a food processor or with a potato masher. Then slowly add broth until you have the desired consistency. Season to taste.

Note: A puréed Basic Potato Soup is an ideal way to make a rich, creamlike soup base without any dairy products or thickeners. Virtually any vegetable can be added to this base, either chopped, sliced, or puréed, to make an endless variety of soups. Any type of stock can be used in place of water. Diced meat, fish, or fowl can be added. Cheese, milk, sour cream, yogurt, or egg yolks can be added to enrich it. Any herbs or spices can be added for flavor.

- • Substitute Basic White Sauce (see p. 109) thinned to desired consistency with milk or stock for Basic Potato Soup.

SERVES 6

Potato Mushroom Soup

2–4 tablespoons butter or oil
4 cups sliced mushrooms
1 recipe Basic Potato Soup (see p. 96)
1 teaspoon celery salt
1 tablespoon parsley
sea salt and pepper to taste

Heat butter or oil in a skillet. Sauté mushrooms until golden brown. Add mushrooms to potato soup. Stir in celery salt and parsley; season to taste.

- • Substitute sliced onions for mushrooms.
- • Substitute for or use in combination with mushrooms any cooked, diced meat, fish, or fowl.

SERVES 6

Potato Spinach Soup $+$ Swiss chard

    3 cups fresh chopped spinach or
       3 packages frozen chopped spinach,
       steamed and drained
    1 recipe Basic Potato Soup (see p. 96)
    1 cup chopped celery, steamed
    ¼ teaspoon nutmeg
    sea salt and pepper to taste
    sour cream for garnish (optional)

Add chopped spinach to potato soup. Stir in celery and seasonings. Cook for 10 minutes. Garnish with sour cream (optional).
This soup may be frozen.

- Substitute 3 cups fresh broccoli florets, steamed and chopped, or 3 cups frozen broccoli for spinach.
- Substitute 3 cups fresh or frozen asparagus for spinach.
- Substitute 1 cup onion, chopped and sautéed, for celery.
- Substitute 1 teaspoon curry powder for nutmeg.
- Substitute yogurt for sour cream.

SERVES 6

Potato Watercress Soup

2 cups fresh watercress, chopped
  (stems and leaves)
1 recipe Basic Potato Soup (see p. 96)
1 teaspoon celery salt

Add chopped watercress to potato soup. Stir in celery salt. Cook for 10 minutes.

- Substitute fresh sorrel for watercress.
- Substitute dark green lettuce leaves (such as romaine or Boston) for watercress.

SERVES 6

Basic Vegetable Stock

2 quarts water
1 large onion, quartered, or 2 leeks
  (white part only), coarsely chopped
4 cloves garlic, whole
2 carrots, coarsely chopped
3 stalks celery, coarsely chopped
2 large potatoes, coarsely chopped
3 sprigs fresh parsley or 1 tablespoon
  dried parsley flakes
1 bay leaf
1 teaspoon dried thyme
6 whole peppercorns
2 tablespoons tamari (see Glossary)
2 vegetable cubes (optional)
sea salt to taste

Place all ingredients in a large stockpot and bring slowly to a simmer. Simmer, uncovered, for 2 hours. Strain broth through a fine sieve or cheesecloth.

This stock may be frozen.

- Substitute tomatoes, zucchini, cabbage, mushrooms, dark green lettuce leaves, celery tops, spinach, beets and beet tops, or kale for any of the above vegetables.

MAKES 2 QUARTS

SALADS

Jerusalem Artichoke Salad

½ pound Jerusalem artichokes
1 medium red onion, chopped
1 medium carrot, grated
2 stalks celery, chopped
2 tablespoons capers

Steam artichokes for 10 to 15 minutes; peel and slice.
Combine with other ingredients and serve, chilled, with Basic, Curried, or Mustard Mayonnaise or Vinaigrette (see pp. 72-76).

- Substitute potatoes or artichoke hearts for Jerusalem artichokes.
- Substitute green or red pepper for red onion.
- Substitute chopped tomato for carrot or celery.
- Substitute olives or pickles for capers.

SERVES 4–6

Bean Salad

1 cup cooked kidney beans
1 cup cooked navy beans
½ pound fresh or frozen green beans,
    steamed

1 medium onion, chopped
1 cup Basic Vinaigrette Dressing (see
    p. 72)
1 tablespoon honey

Place all ingredients in a mixing bowl and toss to combine. Cover and refrigerate for several hours, tossing occasionally.

- Substitute chickpeas, lima beans, black beans, or soybeans for kidney or navy beans.
- Substitute yellow wax beans for green beans.
- Substitute red or green peppers for onion.

SERVES 4–6

Cold Marinated Broccoli

1 bunch fresh broccoli
1 cup Basic Vinaigrette Dressing (see
    p. 72)

Cut broccoli florets into small sections. Slice stems into thin slices. Place broccoli in a bowl with vinaigrette and toss to coat with dressing. Cover and refrigerate for 24 hours before serving.

- Substitute cauliflower, asparagus, or artichoke hearts for broccoli.

SERVES 2–4

Sweet and Sour Cucumbers

2 cups peeled, thinly sliced cucumbers
salted water to cover
½ cup cider vinegar
2 tablespoons oil (optional)
1 tablespoon honey
sea salt and pepper to taste
1 tablespoon fresh chopped dill

Cover sliced cucumbers with salted water and refrigerate for 2 hours. Mix vinegar, oil (optional), honey, and salt and pepper together in a bowl. Add dill. Drain cucumbers and mix thoroughly with dressing. Chill for several hours.

- Substitute sliced zucchini, or sliced tomatoes and thinly sliced onion, for cucumber.
- Substitute lemon juice for vinegar.
- Substitute maple or turbinado sugar for honey.
- Substitute fresh chopped mint, basil, or chives for dill.

SERVES 4

Lentils Vinaigrette

2 tablespoons oil
1 medium onion, chopped
2 cloves garlic, minced
2 stalks celery, chopped
1 cup dried lentils, washed
1 quart water
1 cup Basic Vinaigrette Dressing (see
  p. 72)

Heat oil in a saucepan and sauté onion, garlic, and celery until tender. Add lentils and water. Bring water to a boil and then lower heat and simmer for about a half hour until tender but not mushy.

Drain and allow to cool.

Toss lentils with vinaigrette and chill.

- Substitute green pepper for onion.
- Substitute fresh ginger for garlic.
- Substitute black beans or adzuki beans for lentils.

SERVES 4

Hot Potato Salad

    6 medium potatoes, peeled
    2 tablespoons butter or oil
    1 medium onion, chopped
    2 stalks celery, chopped
    ½ cup chopped dill pickle
    ¼ cup vegetable stock
    ½ cup vinegar
    1 teaspoon honey (optional)
    1 tablespoon mustard
    sea salt and pepper to taste
    dash of paprika

Boil potatoes until tender. Slice while hot.

Heat butter or oil in a skillet and sauté onion and celery until tender. Stir in pickle and remove from heat.

Heat stock, vinegar, honey (if used), and mustard just to the boiling point. Pour hot liquid over potato mixture; add salt and pepper to taste. Serve garnished with a dash of paprika.

- Substitute 4 cups cooked macaroni or brown rice for potatoes.
- Substitute green or red pepper for onion.
- Substitute green olives or capers for pickle.
- Substitute beef, chicken, or any other type of stock for vegetable stock.
- Substitute lemon juice for vinegar.

SERVES 4–6

Salade Niçoise

½ pound fresh green beans, trimmed
  and steamed until tender
2 onions or scallions, minced
1 tablespoon parsley, chopped
1 cup Basic Vinaigrette Dressing (see
  p. 72)
1 head Boston lettuce, washed and
  dried
1 cup tuna
2 ripe tomatoes, cut in wedges —potatoes
1 medium cucumber, sliced
¼ cup pitted black olives
½ cup alfalfa sprouts

Marinate green beans, onions or scallions, and parsley in half the vinaigrette. Refrigerate until chilled. Line a bowl with lettuce leaves. Add marinated mixture and tuna. Decorate with tomato wedges, cucumber slices, olives, and sprouts. Top with remaining vinaigrette.

- Substitute broccoli for green beans.
- Substitute basil for parsley.

- Substitute cabbage for lettuce.
- Substitute any cubed meat, fish, fowl, or tofu (see Glossary) for tuna.
- Substitute sliced boiled potatoes for tomatoes.
- Substitute avocado slices for cucumbers.
- Substitute capers for olives.

SERVES 4

Tabouleh Salad

1½ cups boiling water
1 cup dry bulgur wheat
2–4 scallions, chopped
1 large tomato, peeled, seeded, and
  chopped
6 fresh mint leaves, minced
½ cup Basic Vinaigrette Dressing (see
  p. 72), with ½ teaspoon tumeric
  added

Pour boiling water over bulgur wheat and let stand until all liquid is absorbed and wheat is fluffy and tender. Mix with all other ingredients and chill.

- Substitute onions, garlic, or peppers for scallions.
- Substitute chopped cucumber for tomato.
- Substitute parsley or basil for mint.

SERVES 4

SAUCES

Basic Brown Sauce

    2 tablespoons cornstarch
    2 cups Basic Beef Stock (see p. 83) or
      canned beef stock

Blend cornstarch with 2 tablespoons of cold stock. Beat in remaining stock and simmer for 5 minutes, stirring constantly, until sauce becomes clear and thickened.

- Substitute any meat, fowl, or vegetable stock for beef stock.
- Substitute arrowroot, potato, or rice starch for cornstarch.

MAKES 2 CUPS

Brown Mushroom Gravy

    2 cups Basic Brown Sauce (see p. 107)
    1 cup sliced, sautéed mushrooms

Combine sauce with mushrooms. Heat slowly.

- Substitute sautéed onions for mushrooms.

MAKES 3 CUPS

Brown Caper Sauce

2 cups Basic Brown Sauce (see p. 107)
¼ cup capers

Combine sauce with capers. Heat slowly.

MAKES 2 CUPS

Basic Tomato Paste

2 tablespoons oil or butter (or 1 each)
1 medium onion, minced
2 teaspoons unbleached white flour
3 pounds ripe tomatoes, peeled,
    seeded, and chopped
1 teaspoon honey (optional)
2 cloves garlic, minced
1 tablespoon fresh parsley, chopped,
    or dried parsley flakes
1 bay leaf
sea salt to taste

Heat butter and/or oil in a large saucepan and sauté onions slowly for 10 minutes until tender. Stir in flour and cook slowly for 3 minutes. Stir in tomatoes, honey (optional), garlic, parsley, and bay leaf. Cover pan and cook slowly for 10 minutes. Uncover, stir, and simmer for about 1 hour until thickened and rich. Cook longer if necessary. Remove bay leaf. Season to taste.

This preparation may be frozen.

- Substitute 1 teaspoon cornstarch or arrowroot dissolved in ¼ cup cold water for wheat flour.
- Substitute 1 teaspoon maple syrup for honey.

MAKES 2 CUPS

Basic White Sauce

2 tablespoons butter or oil
2 tablespoons unbleached white flour
1 tablespoon whole wheat flour
2 cups milk, scalded
sea salt and pepper to taste

Heat butter or oil in a heavy-bottomed saucepan over low heat. Stir in flour and cook slowly, stirring until foamy. Do not allow to brown. Remove from heat and pour in scalded milk all at once, stirring briskly with a wire whisk until sauce becomes thick and smooth. Return to medium heat and stir until sauce comes to a boil. Cook for 1 minute, stirring. Season to taste.

Egg yolks or any grated cheese may be added to this sauce to use over steamed vegetables, pastas, or grains. Tomato paste or mustard may also be added.

- Substitute rice or potato flour for wheat flour.
- Substitute chicken, vegetable, or garlic broth for milk.

MAKES 2 CUPS

Horseradish Cream Sauce

¾ cup whipping cream
¼ cup horseradish
1 tablespoon vinegar

Whip cream until peaks form. Fold in horseradish and vinegar. Refrigerate. Serve with cold meats, seafood, or smoked fish.

- Substitute sour cream or mayonnaise for whipped cream.
- Substitute lemon or lime for vinegar.

MAKES 1 CUP

Mustard Sour Cream Sauce

¾ cup sour cream
¼ cup Dijon-style mustard
1 tablespoon vinegar

Mix all ingredients together. Refrigerate. Serve with cold meats, hard-boiled eggs, or salad.

- Substitute whipped cream or mayonnaise for sour cream.
- Substitute lemon or lime juice for vinegar.

MAKES 1 CUP

Curried White Sauce

2 cups Basic White Sauce (see p. 109)
1 tablespoon curry powder (more or
   less to taste)
sea salt to taste

Blend sauce with curry. Add sea salt to taste.

MAKES 2 CUPS

Mustard White Sauce

2 cups Basic White Sauce (see p. 109)
1 tablespoon Dijon-style mustard
sea salt to taste

Blend sauce with mustard. Add sea salt to taste.

MAKES 2 CUPS

Tomato-ey White Sauce

1½ cups Basic White Sauce (see p. 109)
½ cup Basic Tomato Paste (see p. 108)
1 teaspoon fresh, chopped, or dried
   basil, or
1 teaspoon dried oregano
sea salt to taste

Blend sauce with tomato paste and herbs. Add sea
salt to taste.

MAKES 2 CUPS

Cheese White Sauce

1½ cups Basic White Sauce (see p. 109)
½ cup grated cheddar (or any cheese)
¼ teaspoon mustard (optional)
sea salt to taste

Blend sauce with cheese (and mustard, if used). Add sea salt to taste.

MAKES 2 CUPS

Green Sauce

2 cups Basic White Sauce (see p. 109)
3 tablespoons finely minced fresh
   herbs, such as parsley, dill, basil,
   chives
sea salt to taste

Blend sauce with herbs. Add sea salt to taste.

MAKES 2 CUPS

Egg and Lemon Sauce

3 large eggs, separated, at room
   temperature
¼ teaspoon sea salt
3 tablespoons lemon juice

1 teaspoon cornstarch, mixed with 2
   tablespoons stock (optional)
1 cup warm Basic Chicken Stock (see
   p. 87)

Beat egg whites until they form stiff peaks. Beat in yolks, salt, lemon juice, and optional cornstarch (if you want a thicker sauce). Add warm stock slowly, beating constantly until sauce is smooth.

This sauce is excellent served over steamed vegetables, herbed rice, or meat, or it can be eaten as a soup.

* Substitute lime juice or vinegar for lemon juice.
* Substitute arrowroot for cornstarch.
* Substitute any meat, game, fowl, or vegetable stock for chicken stock.

MAKES 1½ CUPS

Peanut Sauce

2 tablespoons oil
¼ cup peanut butter
2 tablespoons unbleached white flour
1 cup hot milk
1 teaspoon tamari (see Glossary)

Heat oil in a saucepan. Beat in peanut butter. Slowly blend in flour. When these are bubbly, remove from heat and pour in hot milk all at once, stirring vigorously with a wire whisk. Add tamari. When mixture is thoroughly blended, return to heat and cook, stirring constantly, until thick and smooth.

Serve over steamed vegetables and Curried or Exotic Lemon Rice (see pp. 153, 156).

- Substitute tahini (see Glossary) for peanut butter.
- Substitute potato or rice flour for wheat.
- Substitute any type of stock for milk.
- Substitute lemon juice for tamari.

MAKES ABOUT 1½ CUPS

Sour Cream and Dill Sauce

1 cup sour cream
2 tablespoons fresh dill
2 teaspoons lemon juice
½ teaspoon celery salt
sea salt and pepper to taste

Mix all ingredients together and serve, chilled, as a dip for raw vegetables or as a salad dressing.

- Substitute yogurt or Tofu Sour Cream (see p. 77) for sour cream.
- Substitute parsley, basil, or chives for dill.
- Substitute cider or wine vinegar for lemon juice.

MAKES 1 CUP

Tomato Horseradish Sauce

1 tablespoon butter or oil
2 cloves garlic, minced
2 cups chopped tomatoes
2 tablespoons Basic Tomato Paste (see p. 108)

1½ cups Basic Beef Broth (see p. 83)
1 bay leaf
sea salt and pepper to taste
2 tablespoons horseradish

Heat butter or oil in a saucepan and cook garlic slowly, over low heat, for 2 or 3 minutes, being careful not to burn it. Stir in tomatoes and tomato paste. Add broth slowly, stirring until thoroughly blended. Add bay leaf and salt and pepper; simmer, partially covered, for 1 hour. Stir in horseradish.

Serve this sauce with any type of burgers, meat loaf, or chops.

- Substitute 2 tablespoons minced shallots, scallions, or chives or ½ green pepper, chopped, for garlic.
- Substitute 1 teaspoon thyme for bay leaf.
- Substitute 1 tablespoon chili powder (or to taste) for horseradish.

MAKES ABOUT 1½ CUPS

MEAT

Sautéed Beef with Spinach

¼ cup tamari (see Glossary)
2 tablespoons cider vinegar
½ teaspoon minced fresh (or
   powdered) ginger
1 tablespoon honey
1 pound beef filet, sliced thin and
   pounded
½ cup peanut oil
2 pounds spinach, shredded

Combine tamari, vinegar, ginger, and honey. Marinate beef slices in mixture for 3 hours at room temperature. Drain and reserve marinade. Heat half the oil in a skillet and quickly sauté spinach for 1 minute, tossing. Remove spinach from skillet and place on a serving dish in a warm oven. Heat remaining oil and sauté beef slices quickly over high heat until brown on both sides. Place beef slices over spinach and top with heated marinade.

- Substitute any meat, poultry, or game for beef.
- Substitute a few drops Tabasco for tamari.
- Substitute lemon juice for vinegar.
- Substitute minced garlic or scallions for ginger.
- Substitute maple syrup or sugar for honey.
- Substitute any type of oil for peanut.
- Substitute shredded celery and carrots for spinach.

SERVES 2–4

Marinated Steak

    ¼ cup lemon juice
    ½ cup olive oil
    1 clove garlic, minced
    1 tablespoon tamari (see Glossary)
    1 pound porterhouse, sirloin, or
        individual steaks

  Mix lemon juice, oil, garlic, and tamari together and place in a shallow pan. Marinate steak in mixture for at least 3 hours at room temperature, turning often.
  Broil steak on a rack on pan, basting often with marinade.

- Substitute any game or fowl for steak.
- Substitute lime juice or vinegar for lemon.
- Substitute any oil for olive.
- Substitute minced shallots, onions, chives, or ginger for garlic.
- Substitute celery salt for tamari.

SERVES 2–4

Sweet-and-Sour Steak

    1 pound sirloin, porterhouse, or
        individual club steaks
    ½ cup peanut oil
    2 medium onions, sliced thin
    1 tablespoon honey
    2 tablespoons tamari (see Glossary)

Slice steak in thin slices. Heat half the oil in a skillet until very hot but not smoking. Brown slices of meat with onion quickly, turning once. Add honey and tamari and stir for 1 minute.

- Substitute any sliced meat, game, or fowl for steak.
- Substitute any type of oil for peanut.
- Substitute sliced peppers for onion.
- Substitute maple syrup or sugar for honey.
- Substitute ¼ teaspoon dry mustard for tamari.

SERVES 2–4

Shepherd's Pie

2–4 tablespoons butter or oil
1 medium onion, chopped
1 pound ground beef
1 teaspoon basil
1 teaspoon parsley
2 tomatoes, chopped
4 medium potatoes, peeled and boiled
  for mashing
2 tablespoons butter (optional)
½ cup milk
sea salt and pepper to taste
½ cup grated cheddar cheese

Preheat oven to 350°.
Heat butter or oil in a skillet and sauté onion until tender. Add ground beef and sauté, breaking it up with a wooden spoon until it has lost its pink color. Stir in herbs and tomatoes. Mash potatoes with butter (optional), milk, and salt and pepper.

Place meat mixture in a casserole or glass pie plate and pour potatoes over meat. Sprinkle cheddar over potatoes and bake in preheated oven for 15 minutes. Place under hot broiler for 1 minute to brown cheese.

- Substitute green or red pepper for onion.
- Substitute ground lamb, veal, or game or cubed tofu (see Glossary) for beef.
- Substitute chopped celery for tomatoes.
- Substitute grated Parmesan cheese, bread crumbs, or ground nuts for cheddar cheese.

SERVES 2–4

Baked Ham with Mustard-Currant Glaze

1 cup currant jelly
¼ cup Dijon-style mustard
½ cup currants
1 medium-sized ham (canned or cured)

Preheat oven to 325°.
If using a canned ham, follow directions on wrapper.
Place ham on a rack in a shallow roasting pan, fat side up. Cured hams take about 20 minutes per pound.
Thirty minutes from the end of baking time, rinse oven heat to 400°. With a sharp knife, score top of ham in a diamond pattern about ¼ inch deep.
Melt jelly in a saucepan over low heat. Stir in mustard. Add currants and bring just to a boil. Remove from heat and spoon or brush over ham. During glazing, baste several times with pan drippings.
Remove from oven and let stand for 15 minutes before slicing.

- Substitute apple jelly for currant.
- Substitute raisins or chopped apple for currants.
- Substitute pork, lamb, chicken, duck, or venison for ham.

Lamb-Stuffed Eggplant

1 medium eggplant
2 tablespoons butter or oil
1 small onion, chopped fine
1 clove garlic, minced
½ pound ground lamb
2 cups chopped tomatoes
3 tablespoons Basic Tomato Paste (see p. 108)
½ teaspoon oregano
½ teaspoon basil
½ cup cooked brown rice
2 tablespoons lemon juice
sea salt and pepper to taste

Preheat oven to 325°.

Wash eggplant and slice in half, lengthwise. Scoop out most of pulp. Set eggplant shells aside and coarsely chop pulp.

Heat 1 tablespoon butter or oil in a skillet and sauté pulp over medium heat until lightly browned, adding more butter or oil if pan becomes dry. Remove eggplant from pan and set aside. Heat the other tablespoon of butter or oil in the skillet and sauté onion until tender. Add garlic and lamb and sauté until lamb has lost its pink color, breaking it up into little pieces with a wooden spoon. Turn off heat and drain fat from pan.

Add tomatoes, tomato paste, herbs, rice, lemon juice, and salt and pepper and combine well.

Fill eggplant shells with lamb mixture. Place in a buttered baking dish and bake in preheated oven for about 45 minutes until shells are tender but not mushy when pierced with a fork.

- Substitute zucchini for eggplant.
- Substitute any meat or fowl for lamb.
- Substitute buckwheat, millet, or couscous for brown rice.

SERVES 2

Stuffed Pork Roast

1 3-pound rib roast of pork
2 cups bread stuffing
1 cup whole cranberries, cooked
6 slices bacon, preferably
    preservative-free

Preheat oven to 350°.

Pound roast thin. Mix stuffing and cranberries together and spread over flat roast. Pull roast up and tie securely. Place in a roasting pan and place strips of bacon across top of roast. Cook in preheated oven for about 1 hour or until meat reaches desired doneness, basting often. Let stand in off oven for 15 minutes before carving.

- Substitute venison for pork.
- Substitute raw sliced apples for cranberries.
- Substitute olive oil or broth for basting for bacon.

SERVES 6–8

Braised Rabbit

1 2-pound rabbit, cleaned and cut into
  serving pieces
½ cup cider vinegar
1 bay leaf
1 medium onion, chopped
⅛ teaspoon dry mustard
¼ teaspoon celery salt
¼ cup flour
Butter or oil for frying
1 tablespoon honey
¼ cup sour cream

Soak rabbit in salted water for 1 hour. Drain and dry.
Mix vinegar, bay leaf, onion, mustard, and celery salt
together in a flat glass dish. Marinate rabbit pieces in
mixture, refrigerated, for 2–3 days, turning occasionally.

Drain and reserve liquid. Dry rabbit pieces and dip
each in flour. Melt butter or oil in a large skillet and
brown rabbit pieces on all sides. Pour off fat and stir in
remaining marinade and honey. Lower heat, cover, and
simmer for about 1 hour until very tender. Mix in sour
cream just before serving.

- Substitute squirrel, mutton, or goat for rabbit.
- Substitute minced garlic or fresh ginger for onion.
- Substitute ¼ cup tamari (see Glossary) for mus-
  tard.
- Substitute maple syrup or sugar for honey.
- Substitute yogurt for sour cream.

SERVES 2

Veal Scallops with Sour Cream and Caper Sauce

2–4 tablespoons butter
2 veal scallops, pounded thin
½ cup sour cream
¼ cup capers

Melt butter in a skillet and sauté veal over medium heat until golden brown on both sides. Remove from pan. If pan has become dry, add 2 more tablespoons butter. When butter is bubbling, turn off heat and stir in sour cream and capers. Pour over veal and serve immediately.

- Substitute any meat, game, poultry, or fish filet for veal.
- Substitute seedless grapes, sliced in half, for capers.
- Substitute yogurt for sour cream.

SERVES 2

Spicy Burgers

1 pound ground beef, pork, or veal (or a combination)
2 tablespoons flour
1 medium onion, chopped
⅛ teaspoon each allspice, nutmeg, and thyme
butter or oil to fry

Mix ground meat with flour, onion, and spices. Form into patties. Heat butter or oil over medium heat in a skillet and sauté patties until brown on both sides. These may also be broiled.

- Substitute ground venison for beef, pork, or veal.
- Substitute bread crumbs for flour.
- Substitute 2 cloves minced garlic for onion.
- Substitute marjoram for thyme.

MAKES 4–5 PATTIES

FISH AND SEAFOOD

Baked Crab Meat

1 pound crab meat
1 cup bread crumbs
2 tablespoons butter or oil, plus 4
   tablespoons butter cut into bits
¼ cup red pepper, chopped fine
¼ cup green pepper, chopped fine
2 teaspoons minced garlic
4 tablespoons fresh lime juice
2 tablespoons fresh chopped parsley
1 teaspoon celery salt
sea salt and pepper to taste

Preheat oven to 350°.

Combine crab meat and bread crumbs in a mixing bowl.

Heat 2 tablespoons butter or oil in a skillet and sauté peppers until tender. Add garlic and cook for 2 minutes, being careful that it does not burn. Remove from heat and stir in lime juice, parsley, celery salt, and salt and pepper. Combine this mixture with crab meat and mix thoroughly.

Place mixture in a buttered 8-inch casserole or pie plate, dot with butter bits, and bake in preheated oven for 30 minutes until golden brown.

- Substitute tuna for crab.
- Substitute onion for peppers.

- Substitute 1 teaspoon fresh minced ginger or powdered ginger for garlic.
- Substitute 2 tablespoons tamari (see Glossary) for lime.

MAKES 2 LARGE OR 4 SMALL SERVINGS

Fish Cakes *or poultry*

2 cups tuna, flaked
1 cup cooked brown rice
1 egg (optional)
1 medium onion, chopped small
1 teaspoon dry mustard
1 cup Tamari Almonds (see p. 79),
   ground fine
2–4 tablespoons butter or oil for frying

Combine tuna, rice, egg, onion, and mustard in a mixing bowl. Form mixture into patties and coat with almonds.

To fry: Heat butter or oil in a frying pan and fry cakes until golden brown on both sides. Drain on paper towels.

To bake: Preheat oven to 350°. Place fish cakes on a cookie sheet and bake in preheated oven until brown and bubbly, about 15 minutes.

- Substitute any cooked fish or poultry for tuna.
- Substitute millet for rice.
- Substitute bread crumbs for almonds.

SERVES 3–4

Fish Kabobs

2 large filets of sole, haddock, or
  flounder
½ cup oil
¼ cup fresh lime juice
1 tablespoon fresh minced ginger or
  powdered ginger
1 teaspoon sea salt
8 cherry tomatoes or 2 tomatoes,
  quartered
8 small mushrooms
8 pearl onions
4 skewers

Preheat oven to 375°.

Cut fish in 2-inch squares. Mix oil, lime juice, ginger, and salt together in a mixing bowl. Add fish squares and marinate, refrigerated, for 2 hours.

Alternate fish squares, tomatoes, mushrooms, and onions on skewers. Place skewers on a cookie sheet and brush vegetables with remaining marinade. Cook in preheated oven, basting several times, for about 15 minutes until fish is fork-tender.

Place under hot broiler for 1 minute to brown. Serve with Curried or Herbed Rice (see p. 153).

- Substitute shrimp, lamb, beef, or any game for fish
- Substitute fresh lemon juice or tamari (see Glossary) for lime.
- Substitute minced garlic for ginger.
- Substitute red or green pepper, eggplant, or zucchini for any of the vegetables.

SERVES 4

Fish Loaf

1 pound lean white fish filets such as
   sole, haddock, or cod
1 cup milk
2 tablespoons cornstarch
2 eggs
pinch of nutmeg
1 teaspoon sea salt
¼ teaspoon pepper
1 cup heavy cream
2 tablespoons soft butter
2 tablespoons fine bread crumbs

Preheat oven to 325°.

Cut filets in small pieces and place in a blender or food processor with milk, cornstarch, and eggs. Blend in nutmeg and salt and pepper. Blend at high speed until mixture is smooth, scraping down sides when necessary. Blend in cream.

Butter bottom and sides of a 5-cup loaf pan or mold and then sprinkle pan with bread crumbs, discarding any that don't stick.

Pour fish mixture into pan and rap pan sharply on a table a few times to get out any air bubbles. Bake in preheated oven for 1 hour or until an inserted knife comes out clean. Let loaf stand for 10 minutes and then run a knife around edges to loosen. Hold a serving platter over top of pan and then invert.

Serve hot with melted butter and lemon wedges, or cold with Sour Cream and Dill Sauce (see p. 114).

- Substitute tuna, crab meat, lobster, or shrimp, chicken or any fowl, or veal for fish.
- Substitute arrowroot for cornstarch.
- Substitute 1 teaspoon curry powder for nutmeg.

SERVES 4–6

Nutty Fish Squares

2 filets of sole, flounder, or haddock
1 egg, beaten
½ cup Tamari Almonds (see p. 79), *breadcrumbs*
   ground
2 tablespoons butter or oil for frying

Cut filets in bite-size pieces. Dip each piece in egg, then coat with almonds. Heat butter or oil in a frying pan and fry fish until golden brown and crisp.
To bake: Preheat oven to 350°. Place fish in a baking dish and bake in preheated oven until golden brown and bubbly, about 15 minutes.

- Substitute boned chicken for fish.
- Substitute any ground nuts or bread crumbs for almonds.
- Substitute milk for egg.

SERVES 2

French-Fried Frog Legs

1 cup flour, seasoned with sea salt and
   pepper
8 frog legs
2–4 tablespoons butter or oil
1 clove garlic, minced
juice of ½ lemon
1 tablespoon parsley

Place seasoned flour in a bag and toss frog legs to coat evenly. Heat butter or oil in a skillet and sauté frog legs until cooked through and golden brown. Remove to a platter. If pan is dry, add 2 more tablespoons butter and sauté garlic lightly. Add lemon juice and parsley and cook for 1 minute. Pour sauce over frog legs.

- Substitute seasoned bread crumbs or ground Tamari Almonds (see p. 79) for flour. Dip frog legs in 1 beaten egg first, then in the crumbs or almonds.
- Substitute chicken legs or wings, or the legs or wings from any game bird.
- Substitute 1 tablespoon fresh ginger, minced, for garlic.
- Substitute 1 tablespoon tamari plus 1 tablespoon cider vinegar for lemon juice.

SERVES 2

Sole Provençal

2 tablespoons butter or oil
1 large onion, sliced thin
½ pound mushrooms, sliced
1 clove garlic, minced
4 ripe tomatoes, chopped
1 tablespoon parsley
1 tablespoon basil
sea salt and pepper to taste

Preheat oven to 350°.

Heat butter or oil in a skillet and sauté onions until tender. Add mushrooms and garlic and continue to sauté until mushrooms are tender, being careful not to burn the garlic. Stir in tomatoes, parsley, basil, and salt and pepper; simmer for 10 minutes.

Place fish filets in a buttered baking dish and pour sauce over them. Bake in preheated oven for 20 minutes until fish is flaky.

- Substitute frog legs, shrimp, or tofu (see Glossary) for fish. These should be sautéed in the pan until lightly browned before adding tomatoes. Then continue recipe.
- Substitute ½ cup stuffed green olives, sliced, for onions and/or garlic.
- Substitute ½ green pepper, chopped, for mushrooms.

SERVES 4

FOWL

Almond Chicken with Lemon Butter

2 boneless chicken breasts, pounded
  flat
1 egg, lightly beaten
½ cup Tamari Almonds (see p. 79),
  ground
2–4 tablespoons butter
juice of ½ lemon

Dip chicken first in beaten egg and then in ground almonds. Melt butter in a skillet and sauté chicken over medium heat until golden brown on both sides. Pour lemon juice over chicken and cook for 1 more minute.

- Substitute any boneless poultry, veal, or fish filet for chicken.
- Substitute milk for egg.
- Substitute any ground nuts or bread crumbs for almonds.

SERVES 2

Barbecued Chicken Breasts

juice of ½ lemon
4 tablespoons Basic Tomato Catsup
  (see p. 82)
1 tablespoon maple syrup
2 boneless chicken breasts, trimmed

Preheat barbecue or grill.

Mix lemon juice, catsup, and maple syrup together. Brush each breast with mixture.

Barbecue until golden brown and firm to the touch, brushing often with sauce.

- Substitute breast of duck, goose, turkey, pheasant, or guinea hen for chicken.
- Substitute vinegar for lemon.
- Substitute tamari (see Glossary) for tomato catsup.
- Substitute molasses or honey for maple syrup.

SERVES 2

Stir-Fried Chicken with Peanuts

2 boneless chicken breasts
2–4 tablespoons oil
6 scallions with green tops, chopped
1 tablespoon fresh ginger, minced
½ cup peanuts
1 teaspoon cornstarch, dissolved in 1
   tablespoon cold water
1 teaspoon honey
2 tablespoons tamari
red or cayenne pepper to taste
   (optional)

Remove skin from chicken and cut into slices. Cut slices into 2-inch-long and ½-inch-wide strips. Heat oil in a wok or skillet and sauté chicken strips, scallions, and ginger until chicken becomes white and firm. Add peanuts and cook for 2 minutes. Mix cornstarch, honey, and tamari and stir well. Add to wok, stirring constantly until ingredients are coated with a light glaze. This dish may be spiced with hot red or cayenne pepper.

- Substitute ¼ cup chopped green peppers for scallions.
- Substitute 2 cloves minced garlic for ginger.
- Substitute 2 cups shrimp or cubed tofu (see Glossary) for chicken.
- Substitute Tamari Almonds (see p. 79) or pine nuts that have been lightly browned in the oven for peanuts.
- Substitute arrowroot for cornstarch.
- Substitute sugar for honey.

SERVES 2–4

Liver (or Mushroom) Pâté

½ pound chicken, duck, or goose liver
4–6 tablespoons softened butter
1 medium onion, finely chopped
1 tablespoon lemon juice
1 tablespoon tamari (see Glossary)
2 tablespoons heavy cream
1 teaspoon basil
½ teaspoon thyme
¼ teaspoon allspice
sea salt and pepper to taste

Trim livers of any fat. Wash and pat dry. Cut in 1-inch squares. Heat 2 tablespoons butter in a skillet and sauté liver and onion until liver has turned light brown but is still slightly pink inside. Remove liver and onion from pan and set aside. Pour lemon juice and tamari into pan and boil for 1 minute, scraping pan with a wooden spoon.

Place liver and onion, pan juices, and remaining ingredients in a blender or food processor and blend until smooth and creamy, scraping sides when necessary. Add more cream, if necessary, to make a puddinglike consistency.

Place pâté in a crock or bowl and refrigerate. Mixture will become firm when chilled.

Serve with crackers or bread, raw, chopped onion, and chopped hard-boiled egg.

- Substitute 1 pound mushrooms, washed and sliced, for liver.
- Substitute 2 stalks celery, chopped, for onion.
- Substitute any type of broth for cream.
- Substitute parsley or rosemary for basil or thyme.
- Substitute mace for allspice.

MAKES 1 CUP

VEGETABLE DISHES

Stuffed Acorn Squash

   1 acorn squash
   1 teaspoon butter or oil plus
      1 tablespoon butter or oil
   1 small onion, chopped
   ¼ cup raisins
   ¼ cup ground Tamari Almonds (see p. 79)
   1 cup cooked brown rice
   sea salt and pepper to taste
   dash of cinnamon

Preheat oven to 350°.

Cut acorn squash in half. Melt butter and brush on each half of squash. Place on a cookie sheet and bake in preheated oven 30–45 minutes until squash is fork-tender. Sauté onion, raisins, and almonds in butter or oil until onion is tender. Add rice; stir for 1 minute. Season to taste. Fill cooked squash with rice mixture. Top with a dash of cinnamon.

- Substitute sweet potatoes or yams for acorn squash.
- Substitute celery for onion.
- Substitute chopped dates or figs for raisins.
- Substitute any other nuts or peanuts for almonds.
- Substitute millet, barley, couscous, or buckwheat groats for rice.

SERVES 2

Broccoli with Bread-Crumb Sauce

1 small bunch fresh broccoli or 2
    packages frozen broccoli
¼ pound butter or oil
1 cup whole wheat bread crumbs
juice of 1 lemon
1 tablespoon parsley
sea salt and pepper to taste

Steam broccoli until tender. Melt butter or oil in a saucepan. Stir in bread crumbs and lemon juice. Add parsley and seasonings. Cook over medium heat until bread crumbs are bubbly and golden brown. Pour over hot steamed broccoli.

- Substitute any bread crumbs for whole wheat.
- Substitute grated Parmesan or Romano cheese for bread crumbs, or use half bread crumbs and half cheese.
- Substitute lime juice for lemon.
- Substitute basil, dill, or oregano for parsley.
- Substitute cauliflower, asparagus, or green beans for broccoli.

SERVES 2 TO 4

Broccoli and Potato au Gratin

½ bunch fresh broccoli or 1 package
   frozen broccoli
2 medium potatoes
½ cup milk
½ cup cheddar cheese, grated
dash of paprika

Preheat oven to 350°.

Steam broccoli until tender. Peel potatoes and boil until tender. Purée potatoes in a food processor, slowly adding milk (or mash them with a masher and beat in milk).

Place broccoli in an ovenproof casserole or pie plate. Pour puréed potatoes over broccoli. Spread grated cheddar over potatoes and bake in preheated oven about 15 minutes, until cheese is brown and bubbly. Sprinkle on a dash of paprika.

- Substitute cauliflower, sliced tomatoes, or asparagus for broccoli.
- Substitute 1 cup Basic White Sauce (see p. 109) for potatoes.
- Substitute water for milk.
- Substitute any kind of cheese, bread crumbs, or ground nuts for cheddar.

SERVES 2

Meatless Chili

2 tablespoons butter or oil
1 large onion, chopped
1 red pepper, chopped
1 green pepper, chopped
2 cloves garlic, minced
6 oz. Basic Tomato Paste (see p. 108)
2 tomatoes, peeled, seeded, and
    chopped
2 cups cooked white beans
2 cups cooked kidney beans
1 tablespoon honey (optional)
1 tablespoon tamari (see Glossary)
2 teaspoons chili powder (or to taste)
a few drops of Tabasco (for more
    hotness!)

Melt butter or oil in a large saucepan. Sauté onion, peppers, and garlic slowly, until tender. Add all other ingredients and simmer for a half hour.

- Substitute apple for onion.
- Substitute celery or corn for peppers.
- Substitute chickpeas, split peas, lima beans, soybeans, lentils, or black-eyed peas for white and kidney beans.
- Substitute maple syrup, fructose, molasses, or date sugar for honey.
- Substitute sea salt or spike for tamari.

CHILI WITH MEAT
Add 1 pound ground beef or other ground meat to onion mixture after onions are tender. Cook until meat is brown.

SERVES 4–6

Stuffed Mushrooms

12 large, firm mushrooms with stems
1 cup Basic Beef Stock (see p. 83)
½ cup raw brown rice
2 tablespoons butter or oil
1 medium onion, chopped fine
½ cup chopped Tamari Almonds (see p. 79)
1 tablespoon parsley
2 tablespoons tamari
½ cup sour cream
2 tablespoons melted butter or oil

Preheat oven to 325°.

Wash mushrooms and remove stems. Bring stock to a boil, add rice, cover, lower heat, and simmer for 35 minutes until most of stock has been absorbed. Uncover and cook for 10 more minutes until grains of rice are dry and separate easily.

Chop mushroom stems. Heat butter or oil in a skillet and sauté stems with onion until they are golden brown. Add almonds, parsley, tamari, and sour cream and blend all ingredients together well.

Brush mushroom caps with melted butter or oil and fill each with filling. Set mushrooms caps on a cookie sheet and bake, covered with foil, in preheated oven for 20 minutes. Remove foil and place under a hot broiler for 1 or 2 minutes to brown tops.

- Substitute ½ cup millet or buckwheat groats cooked in 2½ cups stock for brown rice.
- Substitute any ground nuts or 2 tablespoons sesame seeds for almonds.

- Substitute chopped chives or basil for parsley.
- Substitute yogurt or 1 beaten egg for sour cream.

MAKES 12 MUSHROOMS

Mushrooms Stroganoff

4 tablespoons butter or oil
2 medium onions, chopped
4 cups sliced mushrooms
1 cup beef or chicken broth
2 teaspoons parsley
sea salt and pepper to taste
1 cup sour cream
dash of paprika

Heat butter or oil in a skillet and sauté onions over medium heat until tender. Add sliced mushrooms and sauté until cooked through. Raise heat and pour in broth, parsley, and seasonings. Cook for 5 minutes to reduce broth. Turn off heat and stir in sour cream. Stir well and heat on very low temperature so as to not curdle sour cream.

Serve over noodles or rice with a dash of paprika.

- Substitute green peppers for onions.
- Substitute broccoli for mushrooms. Steam broccoli until stems are tender. Then sauté.
- Substitute vegetable broth for beef or chicken.

SERVES 4

Herbed Soybeans

¼ pound dried soybeans
2 tablespoons butter or oil
1 medium onion, chopped
1 clove garlic, minced
1 teaspoon parsley
½ teaspoon thyme
1 teaspoon dill
2 tomatoes, chopped
2 tablespoons Basic Tomato Paste (see
   p.108)
½ cup grated Parmesan cheese

Wash beans and soak overnight.
Preheat oven to 300°.
Add more water if necessary to cover beans and cook 2–3 hours until beans are tender. Drain and reserve 2 cups cooking liquid.
Heat butter or oil in a skillet and sauté onion until tender. Add garlic and herbs and sauté 2 minutes more. Pour in beans and liquid and allow to simmer until liquid is somewhat reduced, about 10 minutes.
Place beans in a buttered casserole. Stir in tomatoes, tomato paste, and cheese. Cover casserole and bake in preheated oven for 2 hours.

- Substitute any kind of beans (or combination of beans) for soy.
- Substitute green pepper for onion.
- Substitute 1 teaspoon minced fresh ginger for garlic.
- Substitute rosemary, marjoram, or basil for any of the herbs.

- Substitute chopped celery for tomatoes.
- Substitute any type of grated cheese for Parmesan.

SERVES 4–6

Festive Sweet Potato Casserole

1 tablespoon butter or oil
1 large sweet potato or yam, baked,
  peeled, and sliced
1 large tart apple, cored and sliced
1 medium red onion, sliced thin
¼ cup orange juice
1 tablespoon date sugar
¼ teaspoon cinnamon

Preheat oven to 350°.
Heat butter or oil in a glass pie plate or casserole. Alternate slices of sweet potato, apple, and onion. Pour orange juice over all. Sprinkle with date sugar and cinnamon. Bake in preheated oven 15–20 minutes until apple and onion are tender.

- Substitute pumpkin, squash, turnips, or rutabaga for sweet potato.
- Substitute pears or bananas for apples.
- Substitute raisins for onions.
- Substitute apple or pineapple juice for orange juice.
- Substitute allspice, clove, or cardamom for cinnamon.

SERVES 2

Sweet Potato and Banana Soufflé

2 cups cooked mashed sweet potatoes
    or yams
1 large banana, mashed
1 egg, separated
¼ cup milk
¼ teaspoon cinnamon

Preheat oven to 450°.

Combine sweet potatoes or yams, banana, egg yolk, milk, and cinnamon. Beat egg white until stiff and fold into potato mixture. Place in well-buttered individual soufflé cups or drop by tablespoonfuls onto a buttered cookie sheet. Bake 10–15 minutes until golden brown and puffed.

• Substitute yellow squash or pumpkin for sweet potato.
• Substitute ½ cup applesauce for banana.
• Substitute juice for milk.

SERVES 4–6

Fried Zucchini

2 medium zucchini
1 egg, lightly beaten
½ cup ground Tamari Almonds (see p. 79)
butter or oil for frying
1 lemon

Slice zucchini in ½-inch round slices. Dip each slice in beaten egg and then in ground almonds. Heat butter or oil in a skillet. Sauté over medium heat until golden brown on both sides. Squeeze lemon juice over zucchini; cook for 1 minute and serve.

- Substitute eggplant or green tomatoes for zucchini.
- Substitute milk for egg.
- Substitute bread crumbs or flour for Tamari Almonds.

SERVES 2–4

Stuffed Zucchini

1 large zucchini
2–4 tablespoons butter or oil
1 medium onion, chopped
½ cup sliced mushrooms
½ cup Basic Chicken Stock (see p. 87)
½ teaspoon basil
½ teaspoon thyme
2 cups cubed poultry stuffing or bread
   (preferably whole wheat)
salt and pepper to taste

Preheat oven to 350°.
Steam whole zucchini for 15 minutes. Slice in half lengthwise and scoop out most of pulp. Set aside 2 halves of shell and pulp. Heat butter or oil in a skillet and sauté onion until tender. Add mushrooms and zucchini pulp and sauté for 5 minutes. Pour in stock, add herbs, and bring to a boil. Put stuffing or bread

cubes in a large mixing bowl and pour stock and vegetables over it. Mix well. Season to taste. Fill zucchini shells with filling and place on a buttered baking sheet. Bake in preheated oven for about 30 minutes, until stuffing is hot and shells can be easily pierced with a fork.

- Substitute eggplant for zucchini.
- Substitute chopped celery for onion.
- Substitute any type of stock for chicken.

SERVES 2–4

EGGS, CREPES, AND RICE AND PASTA DISHES

Scrambled Eggs with Herbs and Cheese

4 eggs
½ cup cottage cheese
2 tablespoons grated cheddar cheese
1 teaspoon parsley
1 teaspoon chives
sea salt and pepper to taste
2 tablespoons butter or oil

Mix eggs, cheeses, herbs, and salt and pepper together. Heat butter or oil in a skillet and scramble egg mixture to desired consistency.

- Substitute ½ cup any type of sprouts for cheese.
- Substitute 1 small onion or 2 scallions, chopped, for herbs.

SERVES 2

Basic Crepes — *Passover*

½ cup milk
¼ cup water
2 large eggs
½ teaspoon sea salt
2 tablespoons oil
⅓ cup unbleached white flour
⅓ cup whole wheat flour

Place milk, water, eggs, salt and oil in a blender or mixing bowl and blend until smooth. Slowly add flour and blend. Refrigerate, preferably overnight, but for at least 2 hours.

Use a 6-inch crepe pan or skillet. Place over moderate heat and brush lightly with butter or oil. Stir batter before each crepe. Pour ¼ cup batter into hot pan and swirl around until batter coats pan evenly. Cook for 1 minute until you can easily loosen edges of crepe from pan. Turn crepe over and cook for 30 seconds on other side. Crepes can be stacked on a plate and kept warm in the oven until ready to be filled.

- Substitute 1 cup potato starch for white flour and whole wheat flour.

MAKES 15 TO 20 CREPES

Ricotta and Spinach Crepes

2 tablespoons butter or oil
1 large onion, chopped

1 cup spinach, cooked and drained
½ teaspoon nutmeg
sea salt and pepper to taste
1 cup ricotta cheese
1 egg yolk
1 recipe Basic Crepes (see p. 148)

Heat butter or oil in a skillet and cook onion over medium heat until tender. Add spinach, nutmeg, and salt and pepper, and mix well. Combine ricotta and egg yolk and add to spinach mixture. Keep mixture warm over a double boiler while you make crepes.

- Substitute ½ pound mushrooms for onions.
- Substitute chopped broccoli for spinach.
- Substitute cottage cheese for ricotta.
- Substitute 1 cup tofu (see Glossary), puréed in blender or food processor, for ricotta cheese.

SERVES 3–4

Lasagna Primavera

½ pound lasagna (preferably whole
    grain), prepared according to
    directions on package
2–4 tablespoons butter or oil
1 large onion, chopped
1 green pepper, chopped
1 cup eggplant, peeled and cubed
3 cups tomatoes, chopped
½ teaspoon oregano
1 teaspoon basil

sea salt and pepper to taste
1 cup grated Parmesan cheese
2 cups Basic White Sauce (see p. 109)

Preheat oven to 350°.

Cook lasagna according to directions on package.

Heat butter or oil in a skillet and sauté onion and green pepper until tender. Add eggplant and continue to sauté until vegetables are golden brown. Add tomatoes, herbs, and salt and pepper to taste.

Add grated cheese to Basic White Sauce.

Place a layer of vegetables on bottom of a buttered lasagna pan. Pour a layer of cheese sauce on top of vegetables and a layer of lasagna over that. Continue to add layers, ending with a top layer of cheese sauce.

Bake lasagna in preheated oven until bubbly. Place under hot broiler for 1 minute to brown top.

- Substitute layers of brown rice for lasagna.
- Substitute boneless chicken breasts or veal scallops for lasagna. Sauté chicken or veal. Cover with vegetable sauce and then cheese sauce. Place under broiler to brown.
- Substitute mushrooms, garlic, broccoli florets (steamed until tender), zucchini, artichoke hearts (steamed until tender), or spinach for any of the vegetables.
- Substitute parsley for oregano or basil.

SERVES 6–8

Linguini with Pesto Sauce

½ pound linguini or any type spaghetti
or noodles (preferably whole grain)
2 cups fresh basil leaves, packed tight
2 cloves garlic
1 cup olive oil
2 tablespoons pine nuts
1 teaspoon sea salt
½ teaspoon pepper
½ cup grated Parmesan cheese

Cook linguini according to directions on package.

Place basil, garlic, and oil in a blender container and blend. Add pine nuts and blend until smooth, stopping machine occasionally to push ingredients down. Sauce should be thin enough to run off a spoon, so add up to another ½ cup oil if necessary.

Pour sauce into a mixing bowl and stir in salt, pepper, and cheese. When linguini is cooked, drain it, return to the pot, add pesto sauce, and toss with linguini until thoroughly mixed.

- Substitute 2 cups fresh parsley and 2 tablespoons dried basil for fresh basil. Fresh parsley may be used without any basil.
- Substitute any oil for olive oil.
- Substitute walnuts for pine nuts.
- Substitute Romano cheese for Parmesan.

SERVES 2

Baked Macaroni and Cheese with Broccoli

2 cups cooked macaroni (preferably
  whole grain)
1 cup Basic White Sauce (see p. 109)
½ cup grated cheddar cheese
1 egg yolk (optional)
1 cup broccoli florets, steamed
2 tablespoons grated Parmesan cheese

Preheat oven to 350°.

Place cooked macaroni in a casserole. Combine white sauce with cheese (and optional egg yolk). Pour over macaroni. Stir in broccoli. Top with grated cheese and bake in preheated oven for 15 minutes or until bubbly and brown on top.

- Substitute brown rice, millet, or buckwheat groats for macaroni. Use wheat substitution in white sauce.
- Substitute dairy-free white sauce, 3 tablespoons tomato paste, or 1 tablespoon mustard for cheddar cheese.
- Substitute bread crumbs or ground Tamari Almonds (see p. 79) for Parmesan cheese.

SERVES 2

Curried Rice

2 tablespoons butter or oil
1 medium onion, chopped
1 apple, cored and chopped
½ cup raisins
2 cups cooked brown rice
curry powder to taste
2 tablespoons peanuts, chopped

Heat butter or oil in a saucepan. Sauté onion, apple, and raisins until tender. Add rice and mix. Stir in curry powder to taste. Garnish with peanuts.

This rice can be served with Curried White Sauce. (see p. 111)

- Substitute millet, couscous, or barley for rice.
- Substitute green or red pepper for onion.
- Substitute almonds or shredded coconut for peanuts.

SERVES 2–4

Rice and Cheese Croquettes

1 cup cooked brown rice
1 egg
¼ cup grated cheese
1 tablespoon parsley
¼ cup whole wheat bread crumbs
¼ cup whole wheat flour
butter or oil for frying

Combine rice and egg. Add cheese, parsley, and bread crumbs. Form into patties and coat with flour. Heat butter or oil in a skillet and sauté until golden brown on both sides.

- Substitute millet or mashed potatoes for rice.
- Substitute sliced cooked or raw mushrooms for cheese.
- Substitute ground Tamari Almonds (see p. 79) for flour or bread crumbs.

MAKES 8 CROQUETTES

Fried Rice

2–4 tablespoons butter or oil
4 scallions, including green tops, chopped
½ pound mushrooms, sliced
1 clove garlic, minced
½ cup green peas, lightly steamed
1 cup leftover meat, chopped fine
2 cups cooked brown rice
½ cup Basic Beef Broth (see p. 83)
2 tablespoons tamari (see Glossary)

Heat butter or oil in a wok or skillet and stir-fry scallions and mushrooms, tossing with two wooden spoons, until lightly browned. Add garlic, peas, and meat, and stir-fry for 1 minute. Add rice, broth, and tamari and toss until thoroughly combined.

- Substitute ½ green or red pepper, chopped, for scallions.
- Substitute 1 teaspoon minced fresh ginger for garlic.
- Substitute any cooked poultry, game, fish, seafood, or tofu (see Glossary) for meat.
- Substitute any type of broth for beef broth.
- Substitute lemon juice for tamari.

SERVES 4

Herbed Rice with Bulgur Wheat

2 tablespoons butter or oil
1 cup raw brown rice
2 cups boiling Basic Vegetable Stock
  (see p. 99)
1 teaspoon basil
1 teaspoon dill
1 tablespoon parsley
1 teaspoon celery salt
½ cup raw bulgur wheat
1 cup boiling water

Heat butter or oil in a saucepan and sauté rice over medium heat, just until it begins to turn brown. Pour in hot stock and add herbs and celery salt. Return to a boil and then lower heat, cover, and simmer for 35 minutes until most of stock has been absorbed. Remove cover and continue to cook for 10 minutes longer.

Place bulgur wheat in a bowl and pour boiling water over it. Let this soak while the rice is cooking until all the water is absorbed and bulgur is fluffy.

Combine rice and bulgur.

- Substitute ½ cup millet cooked in 1¼ cups stock for either the rice or the bulgur wheat.
- Substitute Basic Chicken or Beef Broth (see p. 83, 87) for vegetable.
- Substitute rosemary, thyme, chives, or oregano for any of the herbs.

MAKES ABOUT 4 CUPS

Exotic Lemon Rice

2 tablespoons butter or oil
1 medium onion, chopped
1 teaspoon mustard seed
2 teaspoons turmeric
1 cup raw brown rice
2 cups boiling Basic Vegetable Stock
  (see p. 99)
1 teaspoon sea salt
juice of 1 lemon
¼ cup currants

Heat butter or oil in a skillet that can be covered. Sauté onion with mustard seed and turmeric slowly, until onion is tender. Add rice and stir well. Pour in boiling stock and add salt, lemon juice, and currants. Cover, lower heat, and simmer for 35 minutes until most of liquid has been absorbed. Remove cover and cook for 5 or 10 minutes more until grains of rice are dry and can be separated with a fork.

This is delicious served with steamed vegetables and Egg and Lemon Sauce (see p. 112).

- Substitute chopped apple for onion.
- Substitute celery seed for mustard seed.
- Substitute cumin or saffron for turmeric.
- Substitute barley or millet for brown rice. If using millet, use 2½ cups boiling stock.
- Substitute any meat or fowl stock.
- Substitute raisins, chopped figs or dates, or slivered almonds for currants.

SERVES 3–4

Spinach and Rice Pilaf—Swss dock

1 pound fresh spinach or 2 packages
   frozen spinach
½ cup olive oil
1 medium onion, finely chopped
¼ cup brown rice
1 tablespoon Basic Tomato Paste (see
   p. 108)
1½ cups water
½ teaspoon mint
sea salt and pepper to taste

Tear fresh spinach into small pieces, or thaw frozen spinach until soft. Heat oil in a 4-quart saucepan and sauté onion over medium heat until golden brown. Add spinach and cook until wilted. Stir in rice and cook for 3 minutes. Dilute tomato paste in 1½ cups water and add to spinach-rice mixture. Add mint, salt and pepper. Cover and reduce heat. Simmer for about 30 minutes until liquid is absorbed and rice is tender.

- Substitute kale, mustard greens, beet tops, or celery and celery tops for spinach.
- Substitute butter or any type of oil for olive oil.
- Substitute barley, buckwheat groats or couscous for rice.
- Substitute 1 tablespoon tamari (see Glossary) for tomato paste.
- Substitute parsley or basil for mint.

SERVES 4–6

PANCAKES, MUFFINS, AND BISCUITS

Basic Pancake Mix

   ½ cup unbleached white flour
   ½ cup whole wheat flour
   2 teaspoons baking powder
   1 teaspoon sea salt
   1 cup milk
   2 eggs
   2 tablespoons oil
   2 tablespoons honey

Combine dry ingredients in a mixing bowl. Slowly add milk. Stir in eggs, oil, and honey. Drop by tablespoonfuls onto a hot, lightly oiled pan or griddle. Turn when bubbles appear.

- Substitute rice, oat, corn, rye, barley, or a combination of any of these flours for wheat.
- Substitute juice or water for milk.
- Substitute 1 teaspoon baking powder and 2 tablespoons liquid for eggs.
- Substitute maple syrup for honey.

SERVES 3–4

Apple Buckwheat Pancakes - *wheatless - rice flour*

½ cup unbleached white flour
½ cup buckwheat flour
2 teaspoons baking powder
1 teaspoon sea salt
1 cup milk
2 eggs
2 tablespoons oil
2 tablespoons honey
½ cup chopped apples
1 teaspoon cinnamon

Combine dry ingredients in a mixing bowl. Slowly add milk. Stir in eggs, oil, and honey. Add apples and cinnamon. Drop by tablespoonfuls onto a hot, lightly oiled pan or griddle. Turn when bubbles appear.

- Substitute rice flour for wheat.
- Substitute juice or water for milk.
- Substitute 1 teaspoon baking powder and 2 tablespoons liquid for eggs.
- Substitute maple syrup for honey.
- Substitute pears or any fruit for apples.

SERVES 3–4

Cheddar Cheese Pancakes

½ cup unbleached white flour
½ cup whole wheat flour
2 teaspoons baking powder
1 teaspoon sea salt
¾ cup milk
2 eggs
2 tablespoons oil
1 tablespoon honey
½ cup grated cheddar cheese

Combine dry ingredients in a mixing bowl. Slowly add milk. Stir in eggs, oil, and honey. Add cheese. Drop by tablespoonfuls onto a hot, lightly oiled pan or griddle. Turn when bubbles appear.

- Substitute half corn meal and half oat flour for wheat.
- Substitute juice or water for milk.
- Substitute 1 teaspoon baking powder and 2 table-spoons liquid for eggs.
- Substitute maple syrup for honey.
- Substitute any cheese for cheddar.

SERVES 3–4

Corn Pancakes

½ cup unbleached white flour
½ cup whole wheat flour
2 teaspoons baking powder

1 teaspoon sea salt
¾ cup milk
2 eggs
2 tablespoons oil
1 tablespoon honey
½ cup cooked corn

Combine dry ingredients in a mixing bowl. Slowly add milk. Stir in eggs, oil, and honey. Mix in corn. Drop by tablespoonfuls onto a hot, lightly oiled pan or griddle. Turn when bubbles appear.

- Substitute half corn meal and half rice flour for wheat.
- Substitute juice or water for milk.
- Substitute 1 teaspoon baking powder and 2 table-spoons liquid for eggs.
- Substitute maple syrup for honey.

SERVES 3–4

Cottage Cheese Pancakes

3 eggs, separated
3 tablespoons whole wheat flour
¼ teaspoon sea salt
1 cup cottage cheese

Beat egg yolks with flour, salt, and cottage cheese. Beat egg whites until stiff. Fold egg whites into cheese mixture. Drop by tablespoonfuls onto a hot, lightly oiled pan or griddle. Turn when underside is golden brown.

- Substitute rye, rice, or barley flour for wheat.
- Substitute ricotta cheese for cottage cheese.

SERVES 3–4

Potato Pancakes

4 large potatoes
1 large onion, chopped
2 eggs
¼ cup whole wheat flour
1 teaspoon sea salt
2–4 tablespoons butter or oil (for frying)

Peel and grate potatoes and squeeze out excess liquid. Combine potatoes and onion with eggs, flour, and salt. Heat butter or oil in a frying pan and drop butter by tablespoonfuls into pan. Sauté until golden brown on both sides. Drain on paper towels.

- Substitute grated zucchini for potatoes.
- Substitute apple for onion.
- Substitute rice or barley flour for whole wheat flour.

SERVES 4

Sweet Potato Pancakes

2 large sweet potatoes or yams
2 eggs
¼ cup whole wheat flour
1 teaspoon sea salt
2–4 tablespoons butter or oil (for
  frying)

Bake sweet potatoes until very tender. Remove skin and purée in a food processor or mash with masher. Beat in eggs, flour, and salt. Heat butter or oil in a frying pan. Drop butter by tablespoonfuls into pan and sauté until brown on both sides.

- Substitute cooked pumpkin or yellow squash for sweet potatoes.
- Substitute rice, rye, or barley flour for wheat.

SERVES 4

Apple Spice Muffins - no flour

½ cup butter or oil, at room
  temperature
⅓ cup maple syrup or maple sugar
1 egg
1 cup applesauce
½ cup chopped apples
2 cups unbleached white flour (or 1
  cup unbleached white flour and 1
  cup whole wheat flour)
1 teaspoon vanilla extract

1 teaspoon baking soda
1 teaspoon sea salt
1 teaspoon cinnamon
½ teaspoon nutmeg
½ teaspoon clove
½ cup raisins

Preheat oven to 350°.

Cream together butter (or oil) and maple syrup (or maple sugar) in a mixing bowl. Beat in egg, applesauce, and apples. Add flour and other ingredients. Pour into a well-buttered cupcake tin and bake in preheated oven until muffins are springy, about 15 minutes.

- Substitute honey for maple.
- Substitute 2 tablespoons apple juice and ½ teaspoon baking powder for egg.
- Substitute 1½ cups rice flour for wheat.
- Substitute chopped dates or figs for raisins.

MAKES 1 DOZEN MUFFINS

Banana Walnut Rice Muffins

2 cups brown rice flour
3 teaspoons baking powder
1 teaspoon sea salt
½ cup chopped walnuts (raisins)
3 tablespoons milk
2 eggs
½ cup maple syrup NONE
1 cup mashed bananas
2 tablespoons oil
1 teaspoon vanilla extract
1 teaspoon nutmeg

Preheat oven to 350°.

Combine flour, baking powder, salt, and nuts in a mixing bowl. Stir in milk, eggs, syrup, and bananas. Add oil, vanilla extract, and nutmeg. Pour into a well-buttered muffin tin and bake in preheated oven until springy.

- Substitute 1½ cups oat flour and ½ cup rolled oats for rice flour.
- Substitute almonds or raisins for walnuts.
- Substitute water or juice for milk.

MAKES 1 DOZEN MUFFINS

Corn Muffins

    1 cup corn meal
    1 cup whole wheat flour - rice
    2 teaspoons baking powder
    ½ teaspoon sea salt
    1 egg, beaten
    ¼ cup oil
    ½ cup molasses
    1½ cups milk

Preheat oven to 400°.

Combine dry ingredients. Combine wet ingredients. Fold wet and dry ingredients together just until blended. Butter a muffin tin and fill three-quarters full with batter. Bake in preheated oven for 20 minutes until muffins are springy.

- Substitute 1 cup rice flour for whole wheat flour.
- Substitute honey for molasses.
- Substitute orange juice for milk.

MAKES 1 DOZEN MUFFINS

Popovers

1 cup unbleached white flour
½ teaspoon sea salt
3 eggs, beaten
1 cup milk
2 tablespoons melted butter

Preheat oven to 450°.
Combine all ingredients in a blender or mixing bowl and blend until smooth.
Butter a muffin tin and heat in oven for 5 minutes. Fill two-thirds full with batter. Bake for 20 minutes, reduce heat to 350°, and bake 10–20 minutes more. Popovers should be very high and puffy.

• Substitute ¾ cup potato starch for white flour.

MAKES 1 DOZEN POPOVERS

Sesame Buttermilk Biscuits

2 cups unbleached white flour
1 tablespoon baking powder
1 teaspoon sea salt
½ cup butter or oil, at room
    temperature
⅓ cup maple syrup or honey
⅔ cup buttermilk
2 eggs
⅓ cup tahini (see Glossary)
2 tablespoons sesame seeds and seeds
    for top

Preheat oven to 350°.

Combine dry ingredients in one bowl. In another bowl, cream together butter (or oil) and maple syrup (or honey). Stir in buttermilk, eggs, tahini, and seeds. Slowly add flour mixture, combining well. Pour into a well-buttered cupcake tin. Sprinkle tops with sesame seeds and bake in preheated oven for about 30 minutes, until firm and golden brown.

- Substitute rice or barley flour for unbleached white flour.
- Substitute water for buttermilk.
- Substitute peanut butter and ground peanuts for tahini and sesame seeds.

MAKES 1 DOZEN BISCUITS

Spicy Buttermilk Muffins

molasses — Wheatless me

FRUIT SWEET APPLESAUCE

1 cup unbleached white flour
1 cup whole wheat flour
1 teaspoon baking powder
½ teaspoon baking soda
½ teaspoon sea salt
½ teaspoon cinnamon
½ teaspoon mace
¼ teaspoon nutmeg
¼ teaspoon ginger
1 egg, beaten
¼ cup oil
½ cup honey
1½ cups buttermilk

Preheat oven to 400°.

Combine dry ingredients. Combine wet ingredients. Fold together just until mixed. Butter a muffin tin and fill three-quarters full with batter. Bake in preheated oven for 20 minutes until springy.

- Substitute rice flour for unbleached white flour.
- Substitute cornmeal for whole wheat flour.
- Substitute molasses for honey.
- Substitute 1 tablespoon curry powder or chili powder for spices.

MAKES 1 DOZEN MUFFINS

BREADS

Basic Whole Wheat Bread

For the Sponge
3 cups lukewarm water (85°–105°)
1 tablespoon (1 package) yeast
¼ cup honey
2 cups whole wheat flour, preferably stone-ground
2 cups unbleached flour

For the Dough
1 tablespoon sea salt
¼ cup safflower oil
¾ cups whole wheat flour
1 cup additional unbleached white flour (for kneading)

For the Top
1 egg
¼ cup water
sesame seeds or poppy seeds

To Mix the Sponge
Pour water into a large mixing bowl (or into an electric mixer with a dough hook). Add yeast and stir to dissolve. Add honey and stir. Add flour, 1 cup at a time, until mixture is a mudlike consistency. Now stir up from bottom and around sides in a circular motion, turning bowl a quarter turn each time. Dough will become stretchy and elastic. This will take about 100 strokes. Cover bowl with a damp towel and set in a

warm (85°–100°), draft-free place (on top of stove over a pilot light, or in an oven that has been turned on low for 5 minutes).

First Rise

Let dough rise for 1 hour. It should have expanded and be bubbly.

To Mix the Dough

Add salt and oil. Fold in with same circular motion, turning bowl and trying not to cut through dough, but to keep it as much in one piece as possible. Continue folding and turning motion as you add flour, 1 cup at a time. When dough begins to come away from sides of bowl, turn it out on a floured work surface. Flour your hands and begin kneading dough, using the heels of your hands to push dough away from you. Then fold dough in half and turn a quarter turn. Keep pushing, folding, and turning, adding additional flour, until dough no longer feels sticky. It should feel elastic and stiff. Fold dough into a ball and pinch seams closed.

Second Rise

Wash out bowl and oil it. Put dough, seam side up, in bowl and then turn seam side down. This will oil top of dough to keep it from getting dry while it is rising. Cover again with a damp towel and set in the same warm place to rise for 1 hour or until it has doubled in bulk. The amount of time it takes may vary with temperature and ingredients.

Third Rise

When dough has doubled in bulk, punch it back down in bowl with your fist about 25 times. Cover and let it rise again until doubled in bulk (45 minutes to 1 hour).

Forming the Loaves

Turn out onto floured surface and knead a few times. If dough feels sticky, add a little more flour. Form dough into a ball and cut in half.

Oil 2 bread pans thoroughly so that loaves won't stick.

Preheat oven to 350°.

Take each ball, knead it a few times, and then press it into a rectangle. Then roll the rectangle into a log shape and pinch seams together. Place, seam side up, in oiled pan and, with your fingers, press dough down into shape of pan. Then turn dough over, seam side down, and press down again. Bread should fill two thirds of the pan.

With a sharp knife or razor blade make 3 lengthwise slits, ½ inch deep, in each loaf. This is to allow steam to escape. You may also invent your own decorative design.

For a golden-brown, crusty top mix egg and water together and brush over top of loaf. Sprinkle with sesame or poppy seeds.

Bake for about 1 hour or until golden brown. Loaf should make a hollow sound when tapped with your knuckles.

MAKES 2 LARGE OR 3 SMALL LOAVES

RYE–SOUR CREAM BREAD

This is wheat- and egg-free.

The Sponge

Use 1 cup sour cream in place of 1 cup water, and use rye flour in place of whole wheat and unbleached white flour.

The Dough
Add 1 tablespoon caraway seeds (optional). Use rye flour in place of whole wheat flour.

The Top
Brush with milk or water.

RYE-OATMEAL BREAD

This is wheat- and milk-free.

The Sponge
Use 2 cups rye flour and 2 cups rolled oats in place of whole wheat and unbleached white flour. Separate 1 egg and beat white until stiff. Fold in yolk and stiff white.

The Dough
Use 2 cups rye flour and 2 cups rolled oats in place of whole wheat flour.

RYE-CORN-MILLET BREAD

This is wheat-free.

The Sponge
Use 2 cups rye flour, 1 cup cornmeal (preferably stone-ground), and 1 cup whole or ground millet in place of whole wheat and unbleached white flour.

Add 1 cup dry milk and 1 egg, separated, with the white beaten stiff.

The Dough
Use 2 cups rye flour, 1 cup cornmeal, and 1 cup whole or ground millet in place of whole wheat flour.

Note: Doughs without any wheat flour are always heavier and will not rise as high. The consistency of the bread will be moist and heavy.

Boston Brown Bread

Wheatless - me + (handwritten)

½ cup cornmeal
½ cup rye flour
½ cup whole wheat flour
1 teaspoon baking soda
½ teaspoon sea salt
⅓ cup dark molasses
1 cup buttermilk
½ cup raisins
water

Mix together dry ingredients. Stir in molasses, buttermilk, and raisins. Butter a 1-pound mold or coffee can and fill three-quarters full with batter. Place buttered foil or wax paper over can and tie or tape firmly in place. Place in a deep pot with 1 inch of water. Bring water to a boil on stove. Cover, reduce heat, and simmer for 3 hours, replacing water when necessary. When bread is cooked, remove from mold or can and cool on a rack. If bread is very moist, place in a 350° oven for 15 minutes.

- Substitute oat flour for cornmeal.
- Substitute rice flour for whole wheat flour.
- Substitute apple juice for buttermilk.

MAKES 1 1-POUND LOAF

Corn Spoon Bread

1 package yeast (1 tablespoon)
1 cup warm water
1½ cups organic cornmeal
1 cup unbleached white flour
1 egg
½ teaspoon sea salt
¼ pound melted butter or oil
2 tablespoons honey

Preheat oven to 350°.

Dissolve yeast in warm water. In a mixing bowl add cornmeal, unbleached white flour, egg, salt, butter or oil, and honey. Beat with a wooden spoon or electric mixer for 2 minutes until blended.

Pour into well-oiled 3¾″ × 7½″ × 2″ bread pan. Place dough in a warm, draft-free spot and allow to rise to just below top of pan. Bake in preheated oven for a half hour. Lower temperature to 250° and continue baking until golden brown. Cool slightly and serve from pan with a spoon.

- Substitute 1 cup rye flour for white flour. (Bread will take longer to rise and will not be as light.)
- Substitute ¼ cup plain yogurt or buttermilk for egg.
- Substitute 1 tablespoon molasses or maple syrup for honey.

MAKES 1 3¾″ × 7½″ × 2″ LOAF

Peanut-Butter Bread

Wheatless me — Oat + Cornmeal

1 package yeast (1 tablespoon)
½ cup warm water
1 teaspoon sea salt
2 eggs, beaten
2 tablespoons honey
3 tablespoons oil
6 tablespoons peanut butter
2½ cups unbleached white flour
½ cup ground peanuts

Preheat oven to 375°.

Dissolve yeast in warm water. In a mixing bowl add salt, eggs, honey, oil, and peanut butter. Beat well with a wooden spoon. Stir in 2 cups flour and beat well until blended. Sprinkle ½ cup flour on kneading surface and pour out dough onto it. Knead until soft, adding more flour until dough is no longer sticky. Shape into a round free-form loaf and oil top. Sprinkle with ground peanuts. Place in a warm, draft-free spot for a half hour. Reshape loaf into a higher round just before placing in oven. Bake 30–45 minutes in preheated oven until golden brown. Cool.

- Substitute ground almonds for peanuts.
- Substitute half oat flour and half cornmeal for white flour.

MAKES 1 LOAF

Overnight Potato Bread

1 package yeast
3 tablespoons honey
¼ cup warm water (100°–115°)
½ cup warm milk
6 tablespoons melted butter or oil
2 teaspoons sea salt
1 egg
½ cup mashed potatoes
3 cups unbleached white flour rye

Dissolve yeast and honey in warm water. Add milk, butter or oil, salt, and egg; mix well. Add potato and mix. Add flour, 1 cup at a time, mixing thoroughly. Continue to stir until dough is stiff. Turn out onto a floured board and knead until dough is smooth and elastic, about 10 minutes. Shape into a ball and place in a large, buttered mixing bowl, turning to coat all sides of dough with butter. Cover bowl tightly and place in refrigerator overnight to rise.

Preheat oven to 375°.

Remove from refrigerator and punch dough down with your fist. Turn out onto a floured board and allow dough to rest for 20 minutes. Knead dough vigorously for 10 minutes. Shape into a round loaf and place on a buttered cookie sheet. Set in a warm, draft-free place to rise until doubled in bulk. This may take up to 4 hours. Bake in preheated oven 40–45 minutes until bread is golden brown and makes a hollow sound when rapped with your knuckles.

- Substitute molasses for honey.
- Substitute ½ cup of water in which potatoes were cooked for milk.
- Substitute rye flour for unbleached white flour.

MAKES 1 FREE-FORM LOAF

CAKES

Creamy Cheese Cake

    3 8-ounce packages cream cheese,
      softened
    4 eggs
    1 teaspoon pure vanilla extract
    ½ cup maple syrup
    1 uncooked piecrust, pressed into a
      9-inch springform pan and
      refrigerated for ½ hour

Preheat oven to 375°.

Beat cream cheese with an electric mixer or wooden spoon until light. Add eggs, vanilla extract, and maple syrup and beat until fluffy.

Pour over crust and bake in preheated oven for 35 minutes.

- Substitute 24 ounces tofu (see Glossary) for cream cheese; eliminate 2 eggs (or all 4).
- Substitute 1½ envelopes gelatin and 1½ cups boiling water for eggs. Pour boiling water over gelatin and stir until dissolved. Mix with vanilla extract and maple syrup. Mix with beaten cream cheese until smooth. Cook piecrust and cool. Pour filling over crust and refrigerate until firm.
- Substitute honey for maple syrup.

MAKES 1 9-INCH CAKE

Carob Chip Cupcakes

6 tablespoons butter or oil, at room
  temperature
½ cup maple syrup or maple sugar
1 egg
¼ cup carob powder (see Glossary)
¼ milk
1½ cups unbleached white flour *barley, rice*
1 teaspoon baking powder
1 teaspoon baking soda
½ teaspoon sea salt
½ cup milk
1 teaspoon pure vanilla extract
½ cup carob chips (from health-food
  store)

Preheat oven to 350°.

Cream butter (or oil) and maple syrup (or sugar)
together in a mixing bowl. Beat in egg. Combine carob
powder and milk. Add to batter. Combine flour, baking
powder and soda, and salt. Add to batter alternately
with milk, blending well. Add vanilla extract and carob
chips. Pour into a well-buttered cupcake tin and bake in
preheated oven until springy, about 20 minutes.

- Substitute honey for maple.
- Substitute water for milk.
- Substitute barley or rice flour for wheat.

MAKES 1 DOZEN CUPCAKES

No-Flour Carrot-Almond Cake

1½ cups carrots, steamed and puréed
6 eggs, separated
⅔ cup maple sugar or syrup
2 tablespoons frozen orange juice
    concentrate
2 cups ground almonds
1 tablespoon grated orange rind
1 teaspoon sea salt
1 tablespoon ground cardamom

Preheat oven to 350°.
Combine puréed carrots with egg yolks and maple sugar (or syrup). Stir in frozen orange juice concentrate, ground almonds, orange rind, salt, and cardamom.

Beat egg whites until stiff. Fold whites into carrot mixture. Pour into a well-buttered pan. Bake in preheated oven until springy, about 45 minutes.

- Substitute sweet potato or pumpkin for carrots.
- Substitute honey for maple sugar or syrup.
- Substitute frozen apple juice concentrate for orange.
- Substitute any ground nuts for almonds.

MAKES 1 9-INCH CAKE

No-Flour Nut Cake *preserved*

1 tablespoon sweet butter, softened
5 egg yolks
¾ cup turbinado sugar
1 tablespoon lemon rind, grated
1 tablespoon lemon juice
½ pound hazelnuts, ground
5 egg whites

Preheat oven to 375°.

Brush an 8-inch-wide by 3-inch-deep springform pan with softened butter.

Beat egg yolks and sugar with an electric beater until thick and pale yellow. Add lemon rind, juice, and nuts; mix well.

Beat egg whites until they form stiff peaks. Fold egg whites gently but thoroughly into mixture. Pour into pan and spread evenly to sides.

Bake in center of preheated oven for about 40 minutes until cake is puffy and sides begin to come away from pan. Turn off heat and leave cake in oven for a half hour. Then remove side of pan and cool on a rack.

- Substitute maple sugar for turbinado.
- Substitute orange or vanilla for lemon.
- Substitute ground almonds for hazelnuts.

MAKES 1 8-INCH CAKE

Orange Poppy Seed Cake

½ cup butter or oil, at room
   temperature
½ cup maple syrup or maple sugar
2 eggs
⅓ cup frozen orange juice concentrate
1 cup milk
2 cups unbleached white flour
¾ teaspoon baking soda
½ teaspoon sea salt
1 tablespoon grated orange rind
1 tablespoon poppy seeds

Preheat oven to 350°.
Cream butter (or margarine) and maple sugar (or syrup) together in a large mixing bowl. Beat in eggs. Add frozen orange juice concentrate and milk. Stir until blended. Add flour, soda, salt, orange rind, and poppy seeds and stir. Pour into a well-buttered cake pan or cupcake tin and bake in preheated oven for a half hour until springy.

- Substitute honey or turbinado for maple.
- Substitute frozen lemon, lime, or apple juice concentrate for orange.
- Substitute rice flour for wheat flour.
- Substitute lemon or lime rind or grated apple for orange.

MAKES 1 9-INCH CAKE OR 12 CUPCAKES

Pineapple Upside-Down Oatmeal Cake

⅔ cup rolled oats
6 tablespoons butter or oil
½ cup maple syrup
1 cup boiling water
2 teaspoons pure vanilla extract
2 eggs, separated
1½ cups oat flour
1 teaspoon baking soda
½ teaspoon sea salt
1 teaspoon cinnamon
½ teaspoon allspice
½ teaspoon clove
6 pineapple rings
½ cup maple syrup
4 tablespoons butter or oil, melted

Preheat oven to 350°.

Place rolled oats, butter (or oil), maple syrup, and boiling water in a bowl for 15 minutes. Add vanilla extract and beat in egg yolks. In another bowl, combine oat flour, baking soda, salt, and spices. Add to rolled-oat mixture and stir. Beat egg whites until stiff and fold into oat mixture. Place pineapple rings around bottom of a buttered cake pan. Combine maple syrup and melted butter (or oil) and pour over pineapple. Pour in batter and bake in preheated oven until springy, about 45 minutes. Allow to cool in pan and then invert into serving plate.

- Substitute honey for maple.
- Substitute ½ teaspoon baking powder and 2 tablespoons water for eggs.
- Substitute apple slices for pineapple.

MAKES 1 9-INCH-SQUARE CAKE

FROSTINGS

Almond Egg White Icing

2 egg whites
½ cup turbinado sugar
¼ teaspoon sea salt
2 tablespoons cold water
1 teaspoon pure almond extract
¼ cup slivered almonds

Beat egg whites, sugar, salt, and water together with an electric mixer or wooden spoon until well blended. Place mixture in top of a double boiler over boiling water and beat with a wire whisk for 3 minutes until stiff. Remove from heat and add almond extract. Beat well and spread on cake or cupcakes. Chill. Sprinkle on slivered almonds.

- Substitute maple sugar for turbinado.
- Substitute vanilla for almond extract.
- Substitute any chopped nuts or coconut for almonds.

MAKES 1 CUP

Banana Cocoa Frosting

¼ pound butter, soft
2 tablespoons sweetened cocoa
1 large banana
¼ teaspoon sea salt

Place all ingredients in a food processor or blender, and blend until smooth.

- Substitute 4 ounces tofu (see Glossary) for butter.
- Substitute sweetened carob powder for cocoa.

MAKES 1 CUP

Basic Cream Cheese Frosting

1 8-ounce package cream cheese, soft
¼ cup honey
1 teaspoon pure vanilla extract

Cream together cream cheese, honey, and vanilla extract in a food processor or in a mixing bowl with a wooden spoon, until very smooth and light.
Spread on cake or cupcakes and refrigerate until firm.

- Substitute maple sugar or syrup for honey.
- Substitute almond extract for vanilla.

MAKES 1½ CUPS

Chocolate Cream Cheese Frosting

1 recipe Basic Cream Cheese Frosting
  (see p. 186)
3 ounces semisweet chocolate, melted

Fold melted chocolate into frosting. Spread on cake or cupcakes and refrigerate until firm.

- Substitute ¼ cup sweetened carob powder mixed with 2–3 tablespoons water for chocolate.

MAKES 1½ CUPS

Cream Cheese Nut Frosting

1 recipe Basic Cream Cheese Frosting
  (see p. 186)
1 cup ground nuts

Fold nuts into frosting. Spread on cake or cupcakes and refrigerate until firm.

- Substitute raisins for nuts.

MAKES 2½ CUPS

Coconut Cream Cheese Frosting

1 recipe Basic Cream Cheese Frosting
(see p. 186)
1 cup pure, unsweetened shredded
coconut

Fold shredded coconut into frosting. Spread on cake or cupcakes and refrigerate until firm.

• Substitute shredded carrots for shredded coconut.

MAKES 2½ CUPS

Tutti-Frutti Cream Cheese Frosting

1 recipe Basic Cream Cheese Frosting
(see p. 186)
1 cup mixed dried fruits, chopped
(such as figs, dates, apricots,
prunes, pineapple, apple)

Fold dried fruit into frosting and spread on cake or cupcakes. Chill.

MAKES 2½ CUPS

Honey Currant Nut Glaze

½ cup honey
¼ cup currants
¼ cup chopped nuts

Melt honey over low heat. Stir in currants and nuts. Pour over cake or cupcakes and refrigerate.

- Substitute maple syrup for honey.
- Substitute chopped dried dates or figs for currants.
- Substitute shredded coconut for nuts.

MAKES 1 CUP

Orange Cream Frosting

    1 cup whipping cream
    2 tablespoons frozen orange juice
      concentrate
    2 tablespoons maple sugar or syrup

Whip cream until stiff. Beat in orange juice concentrate and maple sugar or syrup. Spread on cooled cake and chill.

- Substitute 1 teaspoon peppermint extract for orange juice concentrate.
- Substitute honey for maple sugar or syrup.

MAKES 2 CUPS

Orange Honey Glaze

    ¾ cup honey
    ¼ cup frozen orange juice concentrate
    1 tablespoon grated orange rind

Melt honey over low heat. Stir in frozen orange juice. Add rind. Pour over cake or cupcakes and chill.

- Substitute maple sugar or syrup for honey.
- Substitute lemon or lime for orange.

MAKES 1 CUP

PIES

Coc-oat-nut Piecrust

    ½ cup oat flour
    ½ cup rolled oats
    ½ cup shredded coconut
    ¼ cup ground almonds
    ½ teaspoon sea salt
    1 tablespoon poppy seeds (optional)
    3 tablespoons maple sugar or syrup
    3 tablespoons cold butter or oil
    1 tablespoon ice water (eliminate if
      syrup is used)

Preheat oven to 350°.
Place all ingredients in a food processor or mixing
bowl and blend thoroughly. Press into a 9-inch pie plate
and refrigerate for a half hour before baking in preheated oven for 15 minutes, until golden brown.

- Substitute whole wheat or rice flour for oats.
- Substitute shredded carrots for coconut.
- Substitute any ground nuts for almonds.

MAKES 1 9-INCH PIECRUST

Peanut-Butter Piecrust

1½ cups graham cracker crumbs
3 tablespoons maple sugar or syrup
6 tablespoons crunchy or smooth
    peanut butter (preferably pure,
    unsweetened)

Preheat oven to 300°.
Blend ingredients together in a food processor or mixing bowl. Press into a 9-inch pie plate and refrigerate for a half hour. Bake in preheated oven for 15 minutes until crisp.

- Substitute rolled oats for graham cracker crumbs.
- Substitute honey for maple syrup.
- Substitute cashew butter for peanut butter.

MAKES 1 9-INCH PIECRUST

Ricotta Strawberry Filling

1 tablespoon unflavored gelatin
2 tablespoons water
1 cup ricotta cheese
½ cup turbinado sugar
1 cup strawberries, chopped
1 teaspoon almond extract
½ cup sour cream

Dissolve gelatin in water in a small pot over low heat. Cook for 3 minutes and cool. Mix together ricotta, sugar, strawberries, and almond extract. Add cooled gelatin and sour cream to mixture and blend. Refrigerate until set.

- Substitute maple sugar for turbinado.
- Substitute any berries for strawberries.
- Substitute vanilla extract for almond.

MAKES 2½ CUPS

Avocado-Lime Pie

2 large ripe avocados
4 tablespoons lime juice
2 teaspoons grated lime rind
½ cup honey
½ cup whipped cream
1 9-inch piecrust, baked and cooled

Place avocado, lime juice, rind, and honey in a food processor. Blend until very smooth. Pour into a mixing bowl and fold in whipped cream. Pour into piecrust and refrigerate until firm.

- Substitute 2 cups cooked pumpkin for avocado.
- Substitute lemon or orange for lime.
- Substitute 2 egg whites, beaten stiff, for whipped cream.

MAKES 1 9-INCH PIE

Banana Yogurt Pie

1½ cups yogurt
¼ cup maple sugar or syrup
1 teaspoon cinnamon
1 large banana, sliced
1 9-inch piecrust, cooked and cooled
½ cup shredded coconut, toasted

Mix together yogurt, maple sugar or syrup, and cinnamon. Fold in sliced bananas and pour into piecrust. Sprinkle with toasted coconut and chill.

- Substitute 12 ounces tofu (see Glossary) for yogurt. Purée tofu, maple sugar or syrup, cinnamon, and bananas in a food processor or blender until very smooth. Sprinkle on coconut.
- Substitute honey for maple sugar or syrup.
- Substitute chopped nuts for coconut.

MAKES 1 9-INCH PIE

Pecan Pie

4 tablespoons butter or oil
⅔ cup honey
¼ cup molasses
3 eggs
1 tablespoon pure vanilla extract
1 teaspoon cinnamon
¼ teaspoon nutmeg
¼ teaspoon clove

¼ teaspoon allspice
½ teaspoon sea salt
1 cup broken pecans and ½ cup whole
  pecans
1 9-inch piecrust, prebaked for 5
  minutes

Preheat oven to 375°.

Cream together butter or oil, honey, and molasses. Beat in eggs, 1 at a time. Beat in vanilla extract, spices, and salt. Add broken pecan pieces. Pour into prebaked piecrust and decorate with whole pecans. Bake in preheated oven for about 40 minutes until an inserted knife comes out clean.

- Substitute maple sugar or syrup or turbinado sugar for honey.
- Substitute maple syrup for molasses.
- Substitute frozen orange juice concentrate for vanilla extract.
- Substitute ginger, mace, or cardamom for any of the spices.

MAKES 1 9-INCH PIE

Pumpkin Cloud Pie

1½ cups cooked, puréed pumpkin
2 eggs, separated
⅓ cup honey
2 tablespoons molasses
1 teaspoon cinnamon
¼ teaspoon clove

195

¼ teaspoon nutmeg
¼ teaspoon ginger
1 teaspoon sea salt
1 9-inch piecrust, prebaked for 5
  minutes

Preheat oven to 350°.

Blend pumpkin with egg yolks, honey, molasses, spices, and salt. Beat egg whites until stiff. Fold into pumpkin mixture. Pour into prebaked piecrust and bake for a half hour until set.

- Substitute sweet potato or yam for pumpkin.
- Substitute maple sugar or syrup for honey or molasses.
- Substitute 1 cup milk for eggs.

MAKES 1 9-INCH PIE

COOKIES

Almond Crescents *Passover*

    ¾ cup almonds
    cold water
    ½ cup turbinado sugar
    6 tablespoons rose water (available at
       gourmet shops)
    ½ teaspoon cardamom
    2 eggs
    6 tablespoons sesame seeds

Preheat oven to 375°.

Place almonds in a saucepan and cover with water. Simmer for 30 minutes. Drain and purée in a food processor or blender to a paste, using cooking liquid as needed. Place in a bowl and add sugar, rose water, and cardamom. Knead until smooth. Shape into walnut-sized balls and then roll each ball in the palms of your hands to form a cigar shape about 2½ inches long and thicker in the middle.

Beat eggs well in a small bowl and place sesame seeds on a plate. Dip cookies first in egg and then roll in seeds. Shape into crescents and place on a buttered cookie sheet. Bake in preheated oven for about 45 minutes until golden brown.

- Substitute maple sugar for turbinado.
- Substitute orange juice for rose water.
- Substitute poppy seeds for sesame.

MAKES ABOUT 2 DOZEN COOKIES

Carob Chip Meringue Kisses

2 egg whites
¼ cup maple sugar or syrup
¼ teaspoon sea salt
1 teaspoon pure vanilla extract
½ cup carob chips (from health-food
store)

Preheat oven to 300°.

Beat egg whites until stiff. Beat in sugar, salt, and vanilla extract. Gently fold in carob chips. Drop by tablespoonfuls onto a buttered and floured cookie sheet. Bake for 30 minutes.

- Substitute honey for maple sugar or syrup.
- Substitute raisins or nuts for carob chips.
- Substitute frozen concentrated orange juice for vanilla extract.

MAKES 2 DOZEN COOKIES

Ginger Snaps

3 tablespoons oil
¼ cup honey
3 tablespoons molasses
1 egg
1½ cups whole wheat pastry flour
¼ teaspoon sea salt
½ teaspoon cinnamon
1 teaspoon ginger

Preheat oven to 350.

Cream together oil, honey, molasses, and egg. Mix flour, salt, and spices together and add to liquid ingredients, stirring well. Drop by tablespoonfuls onto a buttered cookie sheet. Flour your fingers and press each cookie down very thin. Bake in preheated oven 10–15 minutes until golden brown.

- Substitute maple syrup for honey.
- Substitute ½ cup water for egg.
- Substitute rye or rice flour for whole wheat.

MAKES ABOUT 3 DOZEN COOKIES

No-Flour Oatmeal Cookies

2 eggs
1 cup maple sugar
2 tablespoons butter or oil, melted
1 teaspoon pure vanilla extract
1 teaspoon sea salt
1 cup shredded coconut
1 cup raw, rolled oats

Preheat oven to 350°.

Beat eggs and sugar together. Stir in melted butter or oil. Add vanilla extract and salt. Add coconut and oats and mix well. Drop by half teaspoonfuls onto a well-buttered cookie sheet and bake in preheated oven for about 10 minutes until golden brown.

- Substitute turbinado sugar for maple.
- Substitute almond extract for vanilla.
- Substitute raisins for coconut.

MAKES ABOUT 4 DOZEN COOKIES

Oatmeal Carrot Cookies

1 cup rolled oats
½ cup oat flour
1 teaspoon baking powder
½ teaspoon sea salt
½ cup maple sugar or syrup
4 tablespoons butter, at room
   temperature
1 egg
1 cup grated carrots —Coconut
¼ cup chopped walnuts
¼ cup raisins
½ teaspoon cinnamon

Preheat oven to 350°.
Combine rolled oats, oat flour, baking powder, and sea salt in a mixing bowl. Beat in maple sugar or syrup, butter, and eggs. Add carrots, walnuts, raisins, and cinnamon and beat until blended. Drop by teaspoonfuls onto an ungreased cookie sheet and bake in preheated oven for 10 minutes, until golden brown. Remove from sheet to cool.

- Substitute ½ teaspoon baking powder and 2 tablespoons juice or water for egg.
- Substitute grated coconut for carrots.
- Substitute chopped almonds for walnuts.

MAKES 3 DOZEN COOKIES

Peanut-Butter Cookies

1 cup maple sugar
½ cup butter or oil
1 egg
1 cup peanut butter (preferably pure,
    unsweetened)
½ teaspoon pure vanilla extract
½ teaspoon sea salt
½ teaspoon baking soda
1½ cups unbleached white flour

Preheat oven to 375°.

Cream together sugar and butter or oil. Beat in egg. Add peanut butter and vanilla extract and mix well. Sift together salt, baking soda, and flour. Add slowly to peanut-butter mixture, combining well. Roll dough into walnut-sized balls and place on a buttered cookie sheet. Press each ball down with a fork. Bake 10–15 minutes in preheated oven until cookies just begin to turn golden brown.

- Substitute turbinado sugar for maple.
- Substitute ½ teaspoon baking powder and 2 table-spoons water for egg.
- Substitute rice flour for unbleached white flour.

MAKES ABOUT 4 DOZEN COOKIES

Pineapple Rice Cookies

1 cup brown rice flour
1 teaspoon baking powder
½ teaspoon sea salt
⅓ cup maple syrup
4 tablespoons butter or oil, melted
1 egg
½ teaspoon pure vanilla extract
3 tablespoons pineapple juice
½ cup chopped pineapple
1 teaspoon cinnamon
½ teaspoon clove

Preheat oven to 350°.

In a mixing bowl combine brown rice flour, baking powder, and salt. Add maple syrup, butter or oil, and egg and stir to combine. Add vanilla extract, pineapple juice, chopped pineapple, and spices and mix until blended. Drop by teaspoonfuls onto a buttered cookie sheet and bake until golden brown, about 15 minutes.

- Substitute half cornmeal and half barley flour for rice flour.
- Substitute ½ teaspoon baking powder and 2 tablespoons liquid for egg.
- Substitute apple juice and chopped apple for pineapple.

MAKES 2 DOZEN COOKIES

CUSTARD, PUDDINGS, AND OTHER DESSERTS

Carob Custard

2 tablespoons sweetened carob
    powder
2 cups milk
4 tablespoons maple syrup
½ teaspoon sea salt
2 eggs

Preheat oven to 325°.

Blend all ingredients together in a blender or mixing bowl. Pour into custard cups and place cups in a pan of hot water. Bake 20–30 minutes until set.

- Substitute chopped nuts for carob.
- Substitute ½ cup orange juice and ½ cup pineapple juice for milk. Omit carob and salt. Use 4 beaten egg yolks instead of 2 whole eggs.
- Substitute honey for maple syrup.

SERVES 4

Bread Pudding

4 cups fresh or stale bread, cubed
3 cups warm milk
3 eggs, separated
½ cup maple sugar
1 teaspoon vanilla extract
¼ teaspoon sea salt
½ teaspoon nutmeg
½ teaspoon cinnamon
¼ cup raisins
hot water

Preheat oven to 350°.

Soak bread cubes in warm milk for 10 minutes. Beat egg yolks, maple sugar, vanilla extract, salt, and spices together. Mix with bread mixture and stir in raisins. Beat egg whites until stiff peaks form, and fold into pudding.

Place in an ovenproof dish and set dish in another dish with a few inches of hot water. Bake in preheated oven for 45 minutes.

- Substitute orange or pineapple juice for milk.
- Substitute honey or turbinado sugar for maple.
- Substitute ½ cup orange marmalade or pineapple chunks for raisins.

SERVES 6–8

Brown Rice Pudding

2 cups cooked brown rice
1¼ cups milk
½ teaspoon sea salt
½ cup maple sugar or syrup
2 teaspoons vanilla extract
4 eggs, beaten
½ cup raisins
1 teaspoon cinnamon
½ teaspoon nutmeg
½ teaspoon clove

Preheat oven to 350°.
Combine all ingredients. Place in a buttered casserole. Set casserole in pan of water in preheated oven and bake until set, about 1 hour.

- Substitute apple juice for milk.
- Substitute honey for maple.
- Substitute chopped dates or figs for raisins.

SERVES 6–8

Carob Pudding

1 recipe Basic Vanilla Pudding (see
   p. 208)
3 tablespoons sweetened carob
   powder
1 teaspoon pure vanilla extract

Prepare Basic Vanilla Pudding and add sweetened carob powder and vanilla extract.

- Substitute any fruit jam for carob.
- Substitute pure almond extract for vanilla.

SERVES 4–6

Indian Pudding

2 cups milk
3 tablespoons yellow cornmeal
2 tablespoons molasses
2 tablespoons honey
2 eggs, beaten
½ teaspoon sea salt
½ teaspoon ground ginger
¼ teaspoon nutmeg
2 tablespoons butter
¼ cup raisins

Preheat oven to 325°.

Bring milk just to the boiling point in a 2-quart heavy-bottomed saucepan. Slowly add cornmeal, stirring constantly with a wooden spoon. Lower heat and simmer, stirring often, until mixture becomes thick and creamy. Add molasses and honey and cook for 5 minutes. Remove from heat and beat in eggs and other ingredients.

Pour into a buttered 2-quart casserole and bake in preheated oven for 1½ hours until inserted knife comes out clean and top is golden brown.

- Substitute apple juice for milk.
- Substitute maple syrup for molasses or honey.
- Substitute cinnamon or allspice for ginger or nutmeg.
- Substitute chopped dates or figs for raisins.

SERVES 3–4

Spicy Millet Pudding

½ cup raw millet
1½ cups water
¼ teaspoon sea salt
¼ cup maple syrup
¼ cup raisins
¼ cup grated coconut
1 teaspoon vanilla extract
½ teaspoon cinnamon
¼ teaspoon nutmeg
¼ teaspoon clove

Preheat oven to 350°.
Bring millet, water, and salt to a boil in a saucepan. Remove from heat and add other ingredients. Pour into a buttered 1-quart casserole or pie plate. Cover and bake in preheated oven for a half hour. Serve warm.

- Substitute honey for maple.
- Substitute chopped dates or figs for raisins.
- Substitute chopped almonds for coconut.

SERVES 4

Ricotta Orange Pudding

1 pound ricotta cheese
2 tablespoons heavy cream
¼ cup maple syrup
2 tablespoons frozen orange juice
    concentrate
¼ cup chopped dates
2 large eating oranges, sectioned
½ teaspoon nutmeg

Combine cheese, cream, maple syrup, and orange juice concentrate. Stir in dates. Refrigerate for 1 hour. Decorate with orange sections and sprinkle with nutmeg.

- Substitute honey for maple.
- Substitute strawberry, raspberry, or blueberry jam for frozen orange juice concentrate.
- Substitute raisins or seedless grapes for dates.
- Substitute fresh or frozen berries for orange sections.
- Substitute cinnamon or allspice for nutmeg.

SERVES 6

Basic Vanilla Pudding

¼ cup cornstarch (Potato starch)
¼ teaspoon sea salt
2¼ cups milk
¼ cup maple syrup
2 tablespoons butter or oil
1 teaspoon pure vanilla extract

Combine cornstarch and salt in a saucepan. Add milk slowly, stirring until smooth. Add maple syrup and cook over medium heat, stirring constantly, until mixture boils. Boil for 1 minute and remove from heat. Stir in butter or margarine and vanilla extract. Pour into dessert cups and chill until set.

- Substitute potato starch for cornstarch. Remove pudding from heat as soon as it has reached a boil.
- Substitute honey for maple syrup.
- Substitute frozen orange juice concentrate for vanilla extract.

SERVES 4–6

Apple Crunch

4 large crisp apples, peeled, cored,
    and sliced
1 tablespoon lemon juice
½ cup raisins
4 tablespoons maple syrup
½ teaspoon cinnamon
¼ teaspoon nutmeg
¼ teaspoon clove

Topping
4 tablespoons butter or oil
4 tablespoons maple syrup
½ teaspoon cinnamon
¼ teaspoon nutmeg
¼ teaspoon clove
1 cup granola
½ cup shredded coconut

Preheat oven to 350°.

Place apples, lemon juice, raisins, maple syrup, and spices in a deep-dish pie plate. Mix well. Heat butter or oil in a saucepan. Add maple syrup and spices and stir. Mix in granola and coconut. Pour topping over apples and press down flat. Bake in preheated oven until apples are bubbly and top is golden brown, about a half hour.

- Substitute pears or blueberries for apples.
- Substitute honey for maple syrup.
- Substitute orange or apple juice for lemon.
- Substitute any dry cereal for granola.

SERVES 4–6

Baked Stuffed Apples

¼ cup raisins
¼ cup chopped walnuts
¼ cup sunflower seeds
4 tablespoons maple syrup
½ teaspoon cinnamon
¼ teaspoon cloves
4 large crisp apples, hollowed out

Preheat oven to 350°.

Combine raisins, walnuts, sunflower seeds, maple syrup, and spices in a mixing bowl. Fill each apple with mixture and bake in preheated oven until apples are tender and stuffing is bubbly.

- Substitute pears for apples.
- Substitute chopped raisins or dates for raisins.

- Substitute any kind of nuts for walnuts.
- Substitute honey for maple syrup.
- Substitute sesame or poppy seeds for sunflower seeds.

SERVES 4

Carob Crepes

Follow Basic Crepe Recipe (see p. 148), but substitute 2 tablespoons sweetened carob powder for whole wheat flour.

Cranberry-Orange Mousse

    2 8-ounce packages cream cheese,
       at room temperature
    2 eggs, separated
    1 cup Raw Cranberry-Orange Relish
       (see p. 81)
    ½ cup maple sugar

Beat cream cheese until light. Beat in egg yolks, one at a time. Beat in Cranberry-Orange Relish and maple sugar.

Beat egg whites until they form stiff peaks. Fold cranberry–cream cheese mixture gently into egg whites. Chill.

- Substitute 1½ teaspoons gelatin in 2 tablespoons cold water, dissolved in ¼ cup boiling water, for cream cheese. Chill gelatin mixture. Double amount of Cranberry-Orange Relish and add to gelatin mixture. Then fold in egg whites.

- Substitute 1 cup whipped cream for egg whites. Eliminate egg yolks.
- Substitute cooked cranberries, any kind of jam, or any crushed fruit, such as apricots, peaches, bananas, or berries, for raw cranberries.

SERVES 6–8

Grape Whip

1 envelope gelatin
¼ cup cold water
1½ cups grape juice
¼ cup maple syrup
1 cup seedless grapes, halved
1 cup whipped cream

Soften gelatin in cold water. Heat grape juice and maple syrup and add gelatin mixture. Stir until gelatin is dissolved.

Pour into a serving bowl and chill until almost set. Fold in halved grapes and whipped cream. Chill until firm.

- Substitute agar-agar for gelatin.
- Substitute apple juice for grape juice.
- Substitute chopped apples for grapes.
- Substitute 2 stiffly beaten egg whites for whipped cream.

SERVES 4–6

CHAPTER 5

Useful Suggestions

LUNCH-BOX SUGGESTIONS

A NOTE ABOUT THE LUNCH-BOX SUGGESTIONS

The lunch box is a very exciting, special place. We can all remember opening it with mouthwatering anticipation. Lunch-box eaters are a captive audience.

In this next section we give you delicious suggestions for your lunch-box audience. If you have doubts about our plans for your lunch-box eaters, give them a try. The compliments you will get when they begin to eat their special lunches will be well worth it.

Children especially may turn up their darling little noses at first, but it is our experience that that won't last for long. Their friends will soon be sniffing and tasting the Peanut Butter, Banana, and Tofu Spread—and offering to swap lunches for the Carob Chip Meringue Kisses. Your biggest problem will be seeing to it that your children have a chance to eat the foods you have prepared.

Recipes that can be found in this book have been marked with an asterisk (*).

WEEK 1

Monday	*Peanut Butter, Banana, and Tofu Spread on *Basic Whole Wheat Bread Carrot sticks *Apple Crunch
Tuesday	*Chicken Noodle Soup *Apple Spice Muffin with *Tutti-Frutti Cream Cheese Frosting Fruit
Wednesday	Cold *Almond Chicken with Lemon Butter Cucumber sticks with *Russian Dressing *Pineapple Upside Down Oatmeal Cake
Thursday	*Corn Chowder *Spicy Buttermilk Muffins with *Tofu Cream Cheese and *Raw Cranberry-Orange Relish Fruit
Friday	Cashew Butter and *Apple Butter on *Overnight Potato Bread Pepper rings *Carob Chip Meringue Kisses

WEEK 2

Monday	*Minestrone *Peanut Butter Bread with *Apple Chutney and cream cheese Fruit
Tuesday	*Basic Whole Wheat Bread with leftover

*Baked Ham with Mustard and Currant
   Glaze and cheese
Fruit and *Pineapple Rice Cookies

Wednesday   *Carrot Soup
             *Boston Brown Bread with *Apple But-
                ter
             Fruit and Ginger Snaps

Thursday   Tuna salad on *Overnight Potato Bread
                with lettuce and sliced tomato
             Fruit and *Almond Crescents

Friday   *Chili Bean Soup
             *Banana Walnut Rice Muffins
             *Indian Pudding

ALLERGIC TIPS

WHEN EATING IN RESTAURANTS

Just because you're allergic does not mean you can't enjoy the pleasurable and "catered to" experience eating in restaurants often provides. There are, however, certain guidelines you should follow in order to avoid the symptoms of your food allergy. Here are some rules I advise my patients to follow when eating in restaurants.

1. *Choose simple restaurants*. Less elegant restaurants are often a better bet for the allergic person than the fancier restaurants. Diners, for instance, offer simple and simply cooked foods. In diners and other modest eating establishments, the cook will often prepare the food *your* way. If you are tempted to eat in fancier restaurants, or if your business life requires it, tell the maître d'that you are very allergic and ask him for his assistance in making certain that you get the food prepared the way you've requested.

2. *Order easily prepared, simple foods.* More complicated foods like casseroles, sauces, and pizzas are more likely to trigger the symptoms of your food allergy.

3. *Do not drink alcoholic beverages* if you don't know how foods are prepared. Alcohol always heightens allergic symptoms. Instead, drink Perrier water, seltzer water, or bottled spring water with a twist of lemon or lime.

4. *Plan ahead if you're on the Rotary Diversified Diet.* Choose restaurants that you know will be able to provide the foods on your diet.

5. *Ask that all sauces, salad dressings, and seasonings be served on the side.* Use intelligent discretion when flavoring your foods.

6. *Ask to be seated in the No Smoking section.*

7. *Avoid restaurants that use gas.* Whether gas is used for cooking or in lighting fixtures, it often induces allergic attacks. Sterno buffets can cause problems, too, so avoid them.

8. *Try to avoid using rest rooms in restaurants.* Disinfectants and other cleaning materials are used in public rest rooms. If you are chemically sensitive, a trip to the rest room could interfere with your dining pleasure.

9. *Request that MSG and other flavor enhancers be kept out of your food.* Most Chinese restaurants use MSG frequently but will refrain from using it when requested.

10. *Avoid fancy desserts.* Instead, select fresh fruits, all-natural ice cream, or plain yogurt.

11. *Be safe.* Always carry Alka-Seltzer Gold or salts and vitamin C, or any other natural remedy that helps relieve your symptoms, just in case they should develop.

WHEN GOING TO COCKTAIL
AND DINNER PARTIES

Many people with allergies make their biggest mistakes at cocktail and dinner parties. Party atmospheres are very conducive to slipping back to bad old habits. Though you may have fun at the party, if you aren't careful you will more than likely regret your actions when the party is over. Here are some tips for not getting caught in the aftermath of party fun.

1. *Call your hostess in advance and explain your special needs.* The prime concern of any good hostess is to make sure her guests enjoy her party. If she is aware that your doctor has prescribed a special diet, there will be no hurt feelings if you avoid some of the foods she has made available. She will probably enjoy the opportunity of helping you stick to your diet.

2. *Carry your own "nibblers" with you to enjoy as you mingle with the guests.*

3. *Follow the applicable tips for eating in restaurants when going to cocktail and dinner parties.*

Tobacco smoke can be a real problem for the allergic person. And nowhere is it more prevalent than at cocktail and dinner parties. Here are some tips for dealing with the problem.

1. *Keep your visit short.* Leave when you first notice the onset of symptoms.

2. *Try invisible nasal filters.* They can be purchased at drugstores. But, again, leave when you feel symptoms starting—or, better yet, before they start. You know your own body, and you know when it is time to call it quits.

3. *Don't go to the party, but don't offend your host.* Tell him the truth about your allergy to smoke. When the problem is discussed openly and in advance, he'll understand if you decline his invitation.

4. *Invite guests to your own home*. If you meet people you enjoy being with, but can't stand the smoke at the party, invite them to your home at a later date. Explain to them that you are allergic to smoke, and that is the reason you must leave early. When they come to your home, a Thank You for Not Smoking sign will tactfully remind them of your allergy.

WHAT TO EAT ON HOLIDAYS

If the holiday celebration is to be in your home, keep the menu *simple* but delicious. Once you develop new and healthier eating habits, preparing a feast for a holiday will become second nature to you. Here is one holiday meal that never fails to please.

THANKSGIVING DINNER

Consommé
Fresh vegetable appetizers (with a yummy dip)

Turkey
(from your health-food store with no preservatives, antibiotics, or self-basting features. The turkeys are delicious!)

Plain sweet potatoes   Steamed vegetables (seasoned properly)

Home mashed potatoes   Gravy (using a flour you're not allergic to or a starch such as arrowroot)

Fresh fruit salad (marinated in its own juices)

and/or

Cheese and nuts

Remember, it is not the amount of food that makes your holiday dinner a success, but the way you plan and prepare it. Texture, seasonings, visual delights, and freshness are important ingredients for a delightful holiday banquet.

If you go out to enjoy your holiday meals, be sure you enforce the rules for eating in restaurants.

COLLEGE TIPS

For some people, going away to college is the first real encounter with freedom of choice. Although this experience can contribute to many new growth experiences, there will be no special person to watch over you or your day-to-day choices of foods. An allergic student is in a position where he must be responsible, maybe for the first time, for guarding against the symptoms of food allergy. Here are some tips for making sure that the college experience will be a time of feeling well.

1. *Try to arrange for living quarters which have cooking facilities.* These facilities often require that a student live off campus. Sometimes, a note from your family physician will offer proof of your need to cook for yourself.

2. *When living on campus, explain your special dietary needs to the person in charge of food service.*

3. *Take advantage of the salad bar.* Many colleges now have salad bars with two of their three daily meals. Fill your plate with the many fresh vegetables from this setup, and avoid the "prepared," starchy, and highly salted regulars on the menu.

4. *Don't fill up on cafeteria food.* Instead, use the nearby markets to stock up on foods of your own choosing for snacking during the day.

5. *Follow the rules under the eating in restaurants section when away at school.*

NUTRITIONAL COOKING METHODS

We have included this section on nutritional cooking methods to allow you greater variety in preparing your meals.

Clay-Pot Cooking. Any roast of meat, or selection of game or fowl, can be cooked to perfection in a clay pot. Chicken, for instance, turns out tender and juicy, with crisp brown skin, when cooked in a clay pot. And no basting is necessary. When cooking a bird, rub the inside with lemon juice, sprinkle with sea salt and pepper, and stuff with a handful of parsley. Rub the outside with a little oil. Cover the pot and place in a cold oven. Turn oven on. (Never place a clay pot in a hot oven, because it will crack.) Set oven at 500° and cook until tender and brown (about 1½ hours for a 3-pound bird). Never use any soap or detergent on a clay pot, as it will retain the soapy taste. Wash it with hot water and a little vinegar or lemon juice.

Poaching. Poaching is a nutritional way of preparing foods, especially if you use the poaching liquid as a sauce or base for a sauce.

Steaming. Steaming is a more nutritional way of cooking than boiling because the juices stay in the food instead of being poured down the drain. You can buy a simple steamer in a hardware or health-food store.

Stir-Frying. A wok is great for stir-frying, but a skillet will do. You'll need two wooden spoons. Heat pan over medium-high heat. Add your cooking oil and heat until it begins to steam. Add your ingredients, adding the ones that will take longer to the wok first. Toss the ingredients in the hot oil continuously with the two wooden spoons, keeping the wok or pan as hot as you can without burning the food. Add more oil as needed. A wok with a cover can also be used as a steamer.

A GLOSSARY OF UNUSUAL PRODUCTS USED IN THIS BOOK

WHAT THEY ARE AND WHERE TO FIND THEM

Grains, flours, beans, and nuts. Some of the ingredients in the recipes may be unfamiliar to you, such as bulgur, wheat, millet, oats, brown rice, couscous, and rice flour. All of these ingredients, plus a great variety of beans and nuts, can be purchased in natural-food stores.

Herbs and spices are tastiest when fresh but can be used successfully when dried. Try to keep a few pots of fresh herbs on your windowsill to snip when needed. The more they're cut, the more they'll grow. Herbs and spices can help to make plain foods more interesting when a sauce or other ingredients must be left out. Refer to the Herbs and Spices Chart on pages 238-243 for helpful information.

Oils and vinegars. There are many different varieties of cold-pressed oils and vinegars available in natural-food stores. They have no preservatives and can be used well in rotary diets. They should be kept refrigerated so they will not become rancid.

Pastas and cereals. Many types of pastas can be found in natural-food stores. Some are made with whole wheat or Jerusalem artichoke flour. Natural cereals with no sugars, salt, or preservatives are also available in natural-food stores.

Sprouts. There are as many different types of sprouts as there are beans and seeds. Any type of bean or seed can be sprouted. You can buy sprouts in natural-food stores and in some supermarkets. You can also buy the beans or seeds and sprout them yourself.

Sugars. Many of the recipes in this book suggest pure maple syrup, maple sugar, date sugar, and many types of honeys and molasses. There are also jams made with fruit and honey which are good sweeteners. Dried, chopped, or fresh fruits can be used in place of sugar. Look for these sweeteners in your natural-food store.

Tahini is a paste made out of crushed sesame seeds. It is very high in protein, and can be obtained at natural-food stores.

Tamari is a naturally fermented soy sauce of a higher grade and concentration than regular Chinese soy sauce. It is used as a seasoning for soups, vegetables, whole grains, salads, sauces, and casseroles. Tamari bought at natural-food stores is free of chemicals or preservatives.

Tofu is soybean curd. It is high in protein and comes in packaged squares, usually preserved in water in refrigerators of natural-food stores or in some markets or delicatessens. When you get it home, rinse it or put it in fresh water in a glass container and then refrigerate. It will keep for several days.

APPENDIX

HIDDEN FOOD ALLERGENS

When a substance is contained in a food product and we do not suspect that it is there, we call that substance a hidden food allergen. In many cases, the substance is not even listed on the label of the food product. For example, the government allows a certain amount of dust in food, but you never see dust listed on a label.

Sugar listed on a label could mean you are eating one of many different foods, as sugar is made from corn, cane, rice, dates, honey, and many different fruits.

The following Hidden Food Allergens Chart will help you to better understand what you are eating. Study it carefully, and always be sure to read labels on all food products.

COMMON SOURCES OF HIDDEN FOOD ALLERGENS

Wheat	Sugar	Formaldehyde
Barley Malt	Beer	Cosmetics, especially
Beer	Catsup	nail polish and
Bologna	Cereals	lipstick
Bouillon	Infant formulas	Milk
Bran	Mayonnaise	Shampoo
Candy	Mouthwash	Soap
Crackers	Salad Dressings	Tea
Cream of Wheat	Salt	
Farina	Toothpaste	
Flours	Wine	
Gin		
Gluten		
Graham		
Gravies		
Hamburger		
Ice Cream (thicken-ing agents)		
Liverwurst		
Macaroni		
Matzos		
Mayonnaise		
Ovaltine		
Pancake Mix		
Pepper (synthetic)		
Postum		
Puddings		
Pumpernickel		
Rye		
Soups		
Vitamin E		
Wheat Germ		
Whiskies		
Yeasts (some)		

Corn	Dust	Food Colorings
Aspirin	Wine	Butter
Bacon		Certain Fruits
Baking Mixes		(e.g., oranges)
Baking Powder		Fruit Juices
Beer		Margarine
Bleached Flours		Mouthwash
Carbonated		Processed Meats
Beverages		Soft Drinks
Chewing Gum		Toothpaste
Cough Syrups		
"Cream of . . ."		
Cereals		
Glue on back of		
Stamps and		
Envelopes		
Gravies		
Instant Coffee		
Instant Teas		
Salad Dressings		
Talcums		
Toothpaste		
Vanilla		
Vitamins		
Zest		

Brewer's Yeast	Chlorine	Baker's Yeast	ECP Tetracycline Antibiotics
B Vitamins	Anything with City Water	Barbecue Sauce	Beef
Beer	Coffee	Brandy	Chicken
Wine	Juices	Buttermilk	Eggs
	Soda	Catsup	Seafood (fish markets and grocery stores treat their ice with antibiotics)
	Tea	Cheese	
	Water	Citrus fruit juices, frozen or canned	
		Cottage Cheese	Turkey
		Gin	
		Horseradish	
		Leavening	
		Malted Products	
		Mayonnaise	
		Mushrooms	
		Olives	
		Pickles	
		Rum	
		Sauerkraut	
		Vinegar	
		Vodka	
		Whiskey	
		Wine	

Milk	Mold	Soy	Egg
Au Gratin Dishes	Cheese	Baby Formulas	Albumin
Baked Goods	Nuts	Breads	Baked Goods
Bologna	Wine	Candy	Bouillons
Butter		Cereals	Hamburger Mix
Cocoa Drinks		Ice Creams	Hollandaise Sauce
Doughnuts		Lecithin*	Ice Cream
Gravies		Lunch Meats	Noodles
Hamburgers		Margarine	Ovaltine
Ice Cream		Mayonnaise (label may only say vegetable oil; you must inquire)	Pancake Flours
Junket			Pretzels
Meat Loaf			Soups
Ovaltine			Tartar Sauce
Sauces		Meat Extender	Wine
Sausages		Milk Substitutes	
Sherbet		Plastics, especially in Ford Cars	
Soups		Pork Link Sausages	
Waffles		Salad Dressings	
Whey		Sauces	

*Lecithin is a
   stabilizer in
   leaded gasoline.

FOOD FAMILY CHARTS FOR USE IN THE ROTARY DIVERSIFIED DIET

Food families are groups of foods having a similar biochemical makeup.

We have listed the following food families for your convenience so that you can better prepare your Rotary Diet.

Some of these foods, you will see, are surprisingly related. For instance, carob, licorice, peanut, and tofu belong to the same family. Eggplant, pepper, tomato, and potato are all members of the nightshade family. Therefore, take note, if you're on the Rotary Diet and eat turtle on Monday, you may not eat alligator until Friday!

PLANT KINGDOM

AGAR FAMILY
  antibiotics
  mushroom
  yeast

APPLE FAMILY
  apple
    apple cider
    apple vinegar
  pear
  quince

ARROWROOT FAMILY
  arrowroot

ARUM
  malanga
  taro, poi (dasheen)

BANANA FAMILY
  banana
  plantain

BEECH FAMILY
  beechnuts
  chestnuts

BIRCH FAMILY
  filbert
  hazelnut
  oil of birch
    wintergreen

BUCKWHEAT FAMILY
  buckwheat
  rhubarb
  sorrel

BUTTERCUP FAMILY
  pawpaw

CACTUS FAMILY
  prickly pear
  tequila

CAPER FAMILY
caper

CAPRIFOLIUM FAMILY
elderberry

CASHEW FAMILY
cashew
mango
pistachio

CITRUS FAMILY
angostura
citron
grapefruit
kumquat
lemon
lime
orange
tangerine
  mandarin orange

COMPOSITE FAMILY
(BELLFLOWER)
absinthe
chamomile
chicory
common artichoke
dandelion
endive
escarole
goldenrod
Jerusalem artichoke
lettuce
oyster plant
safflower
salsify
sunflower
vermouth

CYPERACEAE FAMILY
Chinese water chestnut

EBONY FAMILY
persimmon

GINGER FAMILY
cardamom
ginger
turmeric

GINSENG FAMILY
ginseng

GOOSEBERRY FAMILY
currant
gooseberry

GOOSEFOOT FAMILY
beet
  beet sugar
spinach
Swiss chard

GOURD FAMILY
cucumber
  gherkin
muskmelon
  cantaloupe
  casaba
  honeydew
  Persian melon
  Spanish melon
summer squash
  regular pumpkin
watermelon
winter squash
  large pumpkin

GRAINS (GRASSES)
- bamboo
- barley
- corn
  - grits
  - meal
  - oil
  - starch
  - sugar (syrup)
    - cerelose
    - dextrose
    - glucose
- millet
- oats
- rice
- rye
- sorghum
- sugar cane
  - molasses
- wheat
  - bran
  - farina
  - flour
    - gluten
    - graham
  - germ (oil)
  - semolina
  - triticale
- wild rice

GRAPE FAMILY
- grape
  - brandy
  - champagne
  - cream of tartar
  - raisin
  - vinegar
  - wine

HEATHER FAMILY
- blueberry
- cranberry
- huckleberry
- wintergreen

HOLLY FAMILY
- maté

IRIS FAMILY
- saffron

LAUREL FAMILY
- avocado
  - oil
- cinnamon
- sassafras

LECYTHIS FAMILY
- Brazil nut

LEGUMES
- black-eyed pea
- carob
- chickpea
- garbanzo bean
- gum acacia
- gum tragancanth
- jack bean
- kidney bean
- lentil
- licorice
- lima bean
- mung bean
- navy bean

pea
peanut
pinto bean
soybean
  lecithin
  tofu
string bean

LILY FAMILY
aloe
asparagus
chives
garlic
leek
onion
yucca

MACADAMIA FAMILY
macadamia nuts

MADDER FAMILY
coffee

MALLOW FAMILY
cottonseed
  oil
okra (gumbo)

MAPLE FAMILY
maple sugar
maple syrup

MAYAPPLE FAMILY
mayapple

MINT FAMILY
basil
catnip
Chinese artichoke

horehound
lavender
marjoram
mint
oregano
peppermint
rosemary
sage
savory
spearmint
thyme

MISCELLANEOUS
honey

MORNING GLORY FAMILY
(CONVOLVULUS)
sweet potato
yam
  American
  Chinese
  Indian
  tropical

MULBERRY FAMILY
breadfruit
fig
hop
mulberry

MUSTARD FAMILY
broccoli
brussels sprouts
cabbage
cauliflower
collards
kale

MUSTARD FAMILY
  kohlrabi
  mustard
  rutabaga
  turnip

MYRTLE FAMILY
  allspice
  clove
  guava
  paprika
  pimento

NUTMEG FAMILY
  mace
  nutmeg

OLIVE FAMILY
  olive
    oil

ORCHID FAMILY
  vanilla

PALM FAMILY
  coconut
    oil
  date palm
  dates
  sago

PAPAYA FAMILY
  angelica
  anise
  caraway
  carrot
  celery
  dill
  fennel

parsley
parsnip

PEDALIUM FAMILY
  elderberry

PEPPER FAMILY
  black pepper
  white pepper

PINE FAMILY
  juniper
  piñon nut

PINEAPPLE FAMILY
  pineapple (bromelin)

PLUM FAMILY
  almond
  apricot
  cherry
  nectarine
  peach
  plum
    prune

POMEGRANATE FAMILY
  pomegranate

POPPY FAMILY
  poppy seed

POTATO FAMILY
(NIGHTSHADE)
  belladonna
  chili
  eggplant
  pepper
    capsicum
    cayenne

potato
tobacco
tomato

PURSLANE FAMILY
New Zealand spinach
purslane

ROSE FAMILY
blackberry
boysenberry
raspberry
strawberry

SAPODILLO FAMILY
chicle

SARSAPARILLA FAMILY
sarsaparilla

SOAPBERRY FAMILY
lichi nut

SPURGE FAMILY
Tapioca
cassava meal
yucca

STERCULA FAMILY
cocoa
chocolate
cola
gum karaya

TEA FAMILY
tea

WALNUT FAMILY
black walnut
butternut (white walnut)
English walnut
hickory
pecan

ANIMAL KINGDOM

AMPHIBIANS
frog

BIRDS
duck
goose

chicken (prairie)
grouse

chicken (domestic)
peafowl
pheasant
quail

guinea fowl

turkey

pigeon

CRUSTACEANS
shrimp

lobster

crab
crayfish

FISH
shark

sturgeon
  caviar

tarpon

herring
shad

anchovy

sardine

salmon
  caviar

trout

whitefish
chub

smelt

pike (northern)
muskellunge
pickerel

buffalo
  sucker

carp

bullhead
catfish

eel

scrod
cod
haddock
pollack
tomcod
hake
cusk

mullet
barracuda

bass
  rockfish
grouper
perch

snapper
  tile

grunt

bigmouth black bass
smallmouth black bass
  spotted black bass
sunfish

perch (yellow)
pike (walleye)

bluefish

pompano
amberjack
mackerel (jack)

dolphin

weakfish
croaker
whiting
drumfish

porgy

mackerel
  Atlantic
  Spanish
  king
  frigate

tuna
  bonito
harvestfish
swordfish

butterfish

flounder
halibut

sole

rosefish
ocean perch

puffer

INSECTA
  honeybee

MAMMALS
  opossum

rabbit

squirrel

beaver

whale

dolphin

porpoise

bear

raccoon

lion
tiger

elephant

horse

pig

hippo

llama

deer
elk
moose
caribou (reindeer)

cattle

MAMMALS
- buffalo
- sheep (mutton lamb)
- goat

MOLLUSKS
- scallop
- oyster
- quahog
- clam

- abalone
- snail
- squid
- octopus

REPTILES
- turtle
- rattlesnake
- alligator

HERB AND SPICE CHARTS

The herb and spice charts that follow are designed to help you see at a glance all of the many food–herb/spice combinations. The foods are listed across the top of the chart. The herbs and spices are listed on the left-hand side. We have done taste-test research to determine which of the herbs and spices tastes best with each food. If you find an X in the box where the herb or spice and food join, you will find a delicious combination of food and herb or spice. Using the herbs and spices this way will be a great help when doing a food rotation.

Herbs	Beef	Pork	Lamb	Veal	Game Meats	Chicken and Turkey	Game Birds	Eggs	Fish	Shellfish
Allspice	X				X					
Anise	X		X							X
Basil	X	X		X				X	X	X
Bay Leaf	X	X	X	X	X	X	X		X	X
Caraway	X	X	X	X	X	X	X			
Cardamom		X	X		X	X	X			
Cayenne	X	X	X	X	X	X	X	X	X	X
Celery seed	X	X	X	X	X	X	X	X	X	X
Chili powder	X				X			X		
Chives				X		X		X	X	X
Cinnamon	X	X			X					
Clove	X									
Coriander	X	X		X	X	X	X		X	X
Cumin	X	X	X	X	X	X	X	X	X	X
Dill	X					X	X	X	X	X
Garlic	X	X	X	X	X	X	X		X	X
Ginger	X	X	X	X	X	X	X		X	
Horseradish	X	X	X	X	X	X	X			

	1	2	3	4	5	6	7	8	9	10	11	12	13
Leeks	X	X	X	X	X	X	X	X	X	X	X	X	X
Mace	X	X			X	X	X		X			X	
Marjoram		X	X										
Mint			X	X									
Mustard	X	X	X	X	X	X	X	X	X	X		X	X
Nutmeg	X			X		X		X		X			
Onion	X	X	X	X									
Oregano	X		X	X	X	X	X	X	X	X		X	X
Paprika	X	X	X	X	X	X	X	X	X	X	X	X	X
Parsley	X	X	X	X									
Pepper	X	X	X	X	X	X	X	X	X	X	X	X	X
Poppy					X	X					X		
Rosemary	X	X	X	X	X	X	X	X	X	X	X	X	X
Sage		X	X	X	X	X		X	X	X			
Savory							X						
Scallions	X	X	X	X	X	X	X	X	X	X	X	X	X
Sesame	X	X	X	X	X	X	X	X	X	X	X		
Shallots	X	X	X	X	X	X	X	X	X	X	X	X	X
Tarragon			X		X	X	X	X	X	X	X	X	X
Thyme	X	X	X	X	X	X	X	X	X	X	X	X	X
Turmeric	X		X	X	X	X	X	X	X	X		X	X

Herbs	Artichokes	Asparagus	Beans	Beets	Broccoli	Cabbage	Cauliflower	Carrots	Celery	Corn
Allspice			X		X	X		X	X	
Anise						X	X	X	X	X
Basil			X		X			X	X	X
Bay Leaf	X		X		X		X	X	X	
Caraway				X		X		X	X	
Cardamom			X					X		X
Cayenne	X	X	X		X	X	X	X	X	X
Celery seed	X	X	X	X	X	X	X	X	X	X
Chili powder			X			X		X	X	X
Chives	X	X	X	X	X	X	X	X	X	X
Cinnamon						X		X		X
Clove			X	X		X		X		X
Coriander	X	X			X		X	X		X
Cumin							X	X		X
Dill	X	X	X	X				X	X	X
Garlic	X	X	X	X	X	X	X	X	X	X
Ginger		X	X	X	X	X	X	X	X	X
Horseradish		X	X	X	X	X				
Leeks		X			X			X		
Mace								X		X
Marjoram			X					X	X	

Mint								X		
Mustard		X	X			X	X	X	X	X
Nutmeg		X	X				X	X	X	
Onion	X	X	X		X	X	X	X	X	X
Oregano	X		X	X	X	X	X	X	X	X
Paprika		X	X		X	X	X	X	X	X
Parsley	X	X	X		X	X	X	X	X	X
Pepper	X	X	X	X	X	X	X	X	X	X
Poppy		X	X			X	X	X	X	
Rosemary			X					X	X	X
Sage			X		X		X	X	X	X
Savory	X	X	X		X	X	X	X	X	X
Scallions		X	X		X	X	X	X	X	X
Sesame	X	X	X	X	X	X	X	X	X	X
Shallots					X			X	X	X
Tarragon							X	X	X	X
Thyme		X	X		X	X	X	X	X	
Turmeric			X			X	X	X	X	

Herbs	Cucumber	Eggplant	Mushrooms	Peas	Peppers	Potatoes	Spinach	Squash	Tomatoes
Allspice	X								X
Anise									X
Basil	X	X	X	X	X	X		X	X
Bay Leaf		X	X		X				X
Caraway	X							X	
Cardamom		X	X		X	X	X	X	
Cayenne	X	X	X		X	X	X		X
Celery seed	X	X	X	X	X	X	X	X	X
Chili powder	X	X	X		X	X			X
Chives	X	X	X	X	X	X	X	X	X
Cinnamon									X
Clove	X	X							
Coriander	X	X	X		X	X	X	X	
Cumin	X	X	X	X	X	X		X	X
Dill	X	X	X	X	X	X		X	X
Garlic	X	X	X	X	X	X	X		X
Ginger	X	X	X	X	X	X	X	X	
Horseradish						X			X
Leeks									
Mace	X					X			
Marjoram	X				X	X			X

Herb													
Mint				X					X				X
Mustard	X			X	X		X	X	X	X		X	X
Nutmeg								X					
Onion	X		X	X	X		X	X	X	X		X	X
Oregano	X	X	X	X	X		X	X	X	X		X	X
Paprika	X	X	X	X	X		X	X	X	X		X	X
Parsley	X	X	X	X	X		X	X	X	X		X	X
Pepper	X	X	X	X	X		X	X	X	X		X	X
Poppy											X		
Rosemary			X	X	X		X	X	X	X		X	X
Sage											X		X
Savory	X		X	X	X		X	X	X	X		X	X
Scallions	X	X	X	X	X		X	X	X	X		X	X
Sesame	X	X	X	X	X		X	X	X	X		X	X
Shallots	X	X	X	X	X		X	X	X	X		X	X
Tarragon	X	X	X	X	X		X	X	X	X		X	X
Thyme	X						X	X	X	X		X	X
Turmeric			X										X

INDEX

additives, food, 17, 27
alcohol, 34
allergens, 15
  hidden food (chart),
    224–27
almond chicken with lemon
    butter, 132
almonds, tamari, 79
animal fur and dander, 34, 39,
    44
apple: baked stuffed, 210
  butter, 78
  chutney, 80
  crunch, 209–10
  muffins, spice, 164–65
  pancakes, buckwheat, 160
apricot yogurt shake, 69
artichoke salad, Jerusalem,
    101
artificial colors, 14, 16
avocado: guacamole, 70
  -lime pie, 193
  mayonnaise, 74

asparagus: au gratin, 138
  with bread-crumb sauce,
    137

banana: cocoa frosting, 186
  muffins, walnut rice,
    165–66
  soufflé, and sweet potato,
    144
  yogurt pie, 194
bean salad, 101
beef: burgers, spicy, 123
  marinated steak, 117
  sautéed with spinach, 116
  shepherd's pie, 118–19
  stock, basic, 83
  sweet-and-sour steak,
    117–18
beverages: apricot yogurt
    shake, 69
  fresh mint cooler, 67
  tropical shake, 68
  yogurt fruit shake, 68

biscuits, sesame buttermilk, 167–68
borscht, 84
bran, 17
bread: Boston brown, 174
  corn spoon, 175
  peanut-butter, 176
  potato overnight, 177
  rye-corn-millet, 173
  rye-oatmeal, 173
  rye–sour cream, 173
  whole wheat, basic, 170–72
bread pudding, 204
broccoli: baked macaroni and cheese with, 152
  with bread-crumb sauce, 137
  cold marinated, 102
  and potato au gratin, 138
  stroganoff, 141
brown rice pudding, 205
burgers, spicy, 123
butter, apple or fruit, 78

cabbage soup, hearty, 84
cakes: carrot-almond, no-flour, 181
  creamy cheese, 179
  nut, no-flour, 182
  orange poppy seed, 183
  pineapple upside-down oatmeal, 184
caper sauce, brown, 108
carob: chip cupcakes, 180
  chip meringue kisses, 198
  crepes, 211
  custard, 203

pudding, 205–06
carrot: cake, no-flour almond, 181
  cookies, no-flour oatmeal, 200
  soup, 85
catsup, basic tomato, 82
cauliflower: au gratin, 138
  with bread-crumb sauce, 137
cheese: cake, creamy, 179
  ricotta orange pudding, 208
  ricotta strawberry pie, 192
  sauce, white, 112
chestnut soup, 86
chicken: almond, with lemon butter, 132
  breasts, barbecued, 132–33
  liver pâté, 134–35
  noodle soup, 88
  stir-fried with peanuts, 133–34
  stock, basic, 87
  wings, french-fried, 129–30
chili: bean soup, 89
  meatless or with meat, 139
chocolate: banana cocoa frosting, 186
  cream cheese frosting, 187
chutney: apple, 80
  corn, 80
clay-pot cooking, 220
coffee, 29
college eating, 219

cookies: almond crescents, 197
  carob chip meringue kisses, 198
  ginger snaps, 198
  no-flour oatmeal, 199
  oatmeal carrot, 200
  peanut-butter, 201
  pineapple rice, 202
cooking methods, 220
corn: cheddar chowder, 89
  chutney, 80
  muffins, 166
  pancakes, 161–62
  spoon bread, 175
cottage cheese: pancakes, 162
  scrambled eggs and, 147
  sour cream dip, 70
crab, baked, 125
cranberry: -orange relish, raw, 81
  -orange mousse, 211
  pork, stuffed, 121
cream cheese: cake, 179
  cranberry-orange mousse, 211
  frosting: basic, 186
    chocolate, 187
    coconut, 188
    nut, 187
    tutti-frutti, 188
  tofu, 76
crepes: carob, 211
  ricotta and spinach, 148–49
cucumber: sweet and sour, 103
  tapioca soup, cold, 90

cupcakes, carob chip, 180
currant-mustard glaze, 119

dinner parties, 217–18
dip: cottage cheese and sour cream, 70
  sour cream and dill sauce, 114
dressings, salad: see salad dressings
duck, barbecued breasts, 132
dust, 33, 44

eggs, 29, 30, 45
  scrambled with herbs and cheese, 147
  sauce, and lemon, 112
eggplant, lamb-stuffed, 120
enema, 41, 48
exercise, 42

fasting, 37–43
fish: cakes, 126
  kabobs, 127
  loaf, 128
  sole provençal, 130–31
  squares, nutty, 129
  stock, basic, 91
  tuna, baked, 125
  with lemon butter, 132
food addiction, 15–16
food allergens, hidden (chart), 224–27
food allergy, 27–28
food families, 46, 228–35
food rotation, 21, 44, 49, 50
foods, major allergenic, 30, 46

frog legs, french-fried,
129–30
frostings: almond egg white
icing, 185
banana cocoa, 186
cream cheese: basic, 186
chocolate, 187
coconut, 187
nut, 187
tutti-frutti, 188
orange cream, 189

game, braised, 122
garbanzo soup, 92
garlic: soup, French, 93
stock, basic, 93
glaze: honey currant nut, 188
mustard-currant, 119
orange honey, 189–90
grape whip, 212
gravy, brown mushroom, 107
green beans with
bread-crumb sauce,
137
guacamole, 70

ham, baked with
mustard-currant
glaze, 119
hay fever, 13, 33, 34
herb sauce, 112
herb and spice chart, 238–43
heredity, allergies and, 35
holiday eating, 218–19
horseradish: cream sauce,
110
tomato sauce, 114
hummus, 71

hyperactivity, 13, 28, 35
hypoglycemia, 16

icing, almond egg white, 185
Indian pudding, 206

Jerusalem artichoke salad,
101

lamb: eggplant-stuffed, 120
kabobs, 127
lasagna primavera, 149–50
laxatives, 41, 48
lentils vinaigrette, 103–04
lime pie, avocado-, 193
lunch-box suggestions,
213–15

macaroni and cheese with
broccoli, baked, 152
mayonnaise: avocado, 74
basic blender, 73
cashew butter, 74–75
curried, 75
mustard, 76
meat: baked with
mustard-currant
glaze, 119
braised, 122
burgers, spicy, 123
kabobs, 127
liver pâté, 134–35
marinated, 117
roast stuffed with apples or
cranberries, 121
sautéed with vegetables,
116

scallops with sour cream
  and caper sauce, 123
stuffed eggplant, 120
sweet and sour, 117–18
menu plans: allergy-free
    living, 55–57
  cane-, soy-, and egg-free,
    58–61
  corn- and wheat-free,
    61–63
  for seriously allergic
    people, 52
  yeast- and milk-free, 64–66
milk, 29, 45
millet pudding, spicy, 207
minestrone, 94
mint cooler, fresh, 67
mousse, cranberry-orange,
    211
muffins: apple spice, 164–65
  banana walnut rice, 165–66
  buttermilk, spicy, 168–69
  corn, 166
mushroom: gravy, brown,
    107
  pâté, 134–35
  soup, potato, 97
  stroganoff, 141
  stuffed, 140
mustard: -currant glaze, 119
  mayonnaise, 75
  sour cream sauce, 110
  white sauce, 111

oatmeal: bread, rye-, 173
  cake, pineapple
    upside-down, 184

carrot cookies, 200
cookies, no-flour, 199
onion soup, 95–96
organic food, 18

pancakes: apple buckwheat,
    160
  basic mix, 159
  cheddar cheese, 161
  corn, 161–62
  cottage cheese, 162
  potato, 163
  sweet potato, 164
pasta: lasagna primavera,
    149
  linguini with pesto sauce,
    151
  macaroni and cheese with
    broccoli, baked, 152
pâté, liver or mushroom,
    134–35
peanut sauce, 113
  stir-fried chicken with, 133
peanut butter: banana and
    tofu spread, 78
  bread, 176
  cookies, 201
  piecrust, 192
pecan pie, 195
piecrust: coc-oat-nut, 191
  peanut-butter, 192
pies: avocado-lime, 193
  banana yogurt, 194
  pecan, 194–95
  pumpkin cloud, 195–96
  ricotta strawberry, 192–93
pilaf, spinach and rice, 157

pineapple: cake, upside-down oatmeal, 184
cookies, rice, 202
poaching, 220
pollution, air and water, 19–20
popovers, 167
pork roast, stuffed, 121
potato: and broccoli au gratin, 138
bread, overnight, 177
pancakes, 163
salad, hot, 104–05
shepherd's pie, 118
soup, basic, 96
mushroom, 97
spinach, 98
watercress, 99
psychosomatic illness, 14, 29, 35
puddings: bread, 204
brown rice, 205
carob, 205–06
Indian, 206
millet, spicy, 207
ricotta orange, 208
vanilla, basic, 208–09
pumpkin cloud pie, 195

rabbit, braised, 122
relishes: apple chutney, 80
corn chutney, 80
raw cranberry-orange, 81
tamari almonds, 79
restaurants, eating in, 215–16
rice: cheese croquettes, and, 153–54

curried, 153
fried, 154
herbed with bulgur wheat, 155
lemon, exotic, 156
pilaf, with spinach, 157
pineapple cookies, 202
pudding, brown, 205
stuffed acorn squash, 136
ricotta: crepes, and spinach, 148
orange pudding, 208
strawberry pie filling, 192
Rinkel, Dr. Herbert J., 20, 43
Rinkel Mono-Diet, 21
Rotary Diversified Diet, 20–21, 31, 37–38, 43, 44–45

salad: bean, 101
broccoli, cold marinated, 102
cucumbers, sweet and sour, 103
Jerusalem artichoke, 101
lentils vinaigrette, 103–04
salade niçoise, 105
potato, hot, 104–05
tabouleh, 106
salad dressings: avocado, 74
mayonnaise: basic blender, 73
cashew butter, 74–75
curried, 75
mustard, 76
mustard sour cream sauce, 110
Russian, 73

sour cream and dill sauce, 114

vinaigrette, basic, 72

sauces: basic brown, 107

brown caper, 108

brown mushroom gravy, 107

egg and lemon, 112

green, 112

horseradish cream, 110

mustard sour cream, 110

mustard white, 111

peanut, 113

pesto, 151

sour cream: and caper, 123

and dill, 114

tomato horseradish, 114–15

white: basic, 109

cheese, 112

curried, 111

tomato-ey, 111

seafood: crab, baked, 125

shakes: apricot yogurt, 69

tropical, 68

yogurt fruit, 68

smoking, 22, 34, 40, 43

soap, 40

sole provençal, 130–31

soufflé, sweet potato and banana, 144

soup: borscht, 84

cabbage, hearty, 84–85

carrot, 85–86

chestnut, 86

chicken noodle, 88

chili bean, 89

corn cheddar chowder, 89

cucumber tapioca, cold, 90

egg and lemon, 112–13

French garlic, 93–94

garbanzo bean, 92

minestrone, 94–95

onion, 95–96

potato: 96–97

mushroom, 97

spinach, 98

watercress, 99

sour cream: caper sauce and, 123

dill sauce, and, 114

mustard sauce, 110

tofu, 77

soybeans, herbed, 142

spinach: crepes, ricotta and, 148–49

pilaf, and rice, 157

soup, potato, 98

spread, peanut butter, banana, and tofu, 78

squash, stuffed, acorn, 136

steaming, 220

stir-frying, 220

stock: beef, 83

chicken, basic, 87

fish, basic, 91

garlic, basic, 93

vegetable, basic, 99

stress, environmental, 19, 34, 39–40

sweet potato: casserole, festive, 143

pancakes, 164

pie, 195–96

soufflé, and banana, 144

stuffed, 136

symptoms, food allergy, 13, 14, 16
  mental, 28–29
  physical, 27–28

tabouleh salad, 106
tahini, 222
  sauce, 72
tamari, 222
  almonds, 79
tapioca soup, cold cucumber and, 90
test for food allergy, 31
tofu, 222
  cream cheese, 76
  provençal, 130–31
  sour cream, 77
  yogurt, 77
tomato: au gratin, 138
  barbecued chicken breasts, 132–33
  catsup, basic, 82
  fish kabobs, 127
  minestrone soup, 94–95
  paste, basic, 108
  sauce: horseradish and, 114–15
    tomato-ey, 111
  sole provençal, 130
tuna cakes, 126

vanilla pudding, basic, 208–09

veal: burgers, spicy, 133–34
  scallops with sour cream and caper sauce, 123
  with lemon butter, 132
venison, baked, 120
  burgers, spicy, 123–24
vinaigrette, basic, 72
vitamins and minerals, 33, 42
  B_6, 33
  C, 33
  E, 17

watercress soup, potato and, 99
water, spring, 33, 37, 39, 41, 45, 48
wheat, 29, 45
  bulgur with herbed rice, 155
whip, grape, 212
withdrawal, 16, 27, 30, 41

yams: pie, 195–96
  stuffed, 136
yeast, 42
yoga, 45
yogurt: apricot shake, 69
  banana pie, 194
  fruit shake, 68
  tahini sauce, 72
  tofu, 77

zucchini: fried, 144–45
  stuffed: 145–46
    with meat, 121